Praise for *An Uncommon Guide to Retirement*

Most of life is pretty autobiographical, and it cannot not be—which makes for a good question: Why this book? Its thoughtful and gifted author, Jeff Haanen, seems years away from the time when most wonder about the "third third" of life. But in reading *An Uncommon Guide to Retirement*, what is impressive is that he pays attention very well, listening to people and watching the world, wanting to make sense of all of life for all of us. As he does that, he is never far from his own life as a son, a grandson, and a great-grandson, the legacy of long-loved loves a lens for the serious study that brings his book into being. With the growing population of men and women coming into their retirement, I hope that Haanen's good work will be "an uncommon guide" for many, its rich reading of the idea of calling threading its way through the years of life for everyone everywhere.

STEVEN GARBER
Professor of Marketplace Theology at Regent College
Author of *Visions of Vocation: Common Grace for the Common Good*

Haanen does an excellent job describing and then countering the prevailing cultural narratives on retirement. This is a must-read resource for older believers and for the congregational leaders serving them.

AMY L. SHERMAN
Author, *Kingdom Calling: Vocational Stewardship for the Common Good*

Finding the place where God's fire burns in your heart to serve your neighbor and bring joy to your own life—here is the task for those of us entering retirement. I'm convinced Jeff's book, *An Uncommon Guide to Retirement*, is a great resource for those who want to challenge cultural assumptions about retirement and find new ways to serve God for a lifetime.

BRADFORD HEWITT
Retired CEO of Thrivent Financial

I've wanted to be older all my life. It was always in the back of my mind that something was waiting for me there. Jeff Haanen's book might make some uncomfortable, but it has only confirmed what I thought to be true: something good is waiting for all of us.

FRED SMITH
Founder of The Gathering

This is the most comprehensive treatment of retirement from a Christian perspective that I've seen yet. Haanen's counsel is wisdom for adults of every generation today: not only for current retirees and boomers, but also for Gen Xers and millennials, whose choices now will dramatically impact their flourishing in life's latter years.

ANDY OLSEN
Managing Editor at *Christianity Today* magazine

I've had the privilege of working with individuals, families, and couples over the last 40+ years. One of the most difficult areas to deal with is retirement. Our culture teaches us that we can retire to a life of leisure. My counsel has always been: "You're not finished with God's work until he takes you home, therefore let's talk about 'rehirement' instead of retirement." Jeff has made a very meaningful contribution to this topic, one that is desperately needed to be understood by the body of Christ.

RON BLUE
Founder of Kingdom Advisors and Ronald Blue & Co.
Cofounder of National Christian Foundation

An Uncommon Guide to Retirement

FINDING GOD'S PURPOSE FOR THE NEXT SEASON OF LIFE

JEFF HAANEN

MOODY PUBLISHERS

CHICAGO

All Scripture quotations, unless otherwise indicated, are taken from the Holy Bible, New International Version®, NIV®. Copyright © 1973, 1978, 1984, 2011 by Biblica, Inc.™ Used by permission of Zondervan. All rights reserved worldwide. www.zondervan.com. The "NIV" and "New International Version" are trademarks registered in the United States Patent and Trademark Office by Biblica, Inc.™

Scripture quotations marked esv are from The Holy Bible, English Standard Version® (ESV®), copyright © 2001 by Crossway, a publishing ministry of Good News Publishers. Used by permission. All rights reserved.

Scripture quotations marked nasb are taken from the New American Standard Bible®, Copyright © 1960, 1962, 1963, 1968, 1971, 1972, 1973, 1975, 1977, 1995 by The Lockman Foundation. Used by permission. (www.Lockman.org).

Scripture quotations marked kjv are taken from the King James Version.

All emphasis in Scripture has been added.

Names and details of some stories have been changed to protect the privacy of individuals.

Published in association with the literary agency of Wolgemuth & Associates

Edited by Amanda Cleary Eastep
Interior design: Ragont Design
Cover design: Christopher Tobias
Cover illustrations of wave pattern copyright © 2018 by toodtuphoto / Adobe Stock (110008371). All rights reserved.

Library of Congress Cataloging-in-Publication Data

Names: Haanen, Jeff, author.
Title: An uncommon guide to retirement : finding God's purpose for the next season of life / Jeff Haanen.
Description: Chicago : Moody Publishers, 2019. | Includes bibliographical references.
Identifiers: LCCN 2019004707 (print) | LCCN 2019011764 (ebook) | ISBN 9780802497635 () | ISBN 9780802418920
Subjects: LCSH: Retirees--Religious life. | Older people--Religious life.
Classification: LCC BV4596.R47 (ebook) | LCC BV4596.R47 H33 2019 (print) | DDC 248.8/5--dc23
LC record available at https://lccn.loc.gov/2019004707

ISBN-13: 978-0-8024-1892-0

All websites and phone numbers listed herein are accurate at the time of publication but may change in the future or cease to exist. The listing of website references and resources does not imply publisher endorsement of the site's entire contents. Groups and organizations are listed for informational purposes, and listing does not imply publisher endorsement of their activities.

We hope you enjoy this book from Moody Publishers. Our goal is to provide high-quality, thought-provoking books and products that connect truth to your real needs and challenges. For more information on other books and products written and produced from a biblical perspective, go to www.moodypublishers.com or write to:

Moody Publishers
820 N. LaSalle Boulevard
Chicago, IL 60610

3 5 7 9 10 8 6 4 2

Printed in the United States of America

To Mom and Dad.
May your retirement be filled
with the life that is truly life.

Contents

Part I:
RENEWAL

Part II:
WISDOM

Part I:

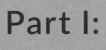

RENEWAL

Chapter 1

Culture

The righteous flourish like the palm tree and grow like a cedar in Lebanon. They are planted in the house of the Lord*; they flourish in the courts of our God. They still bear fruit in old age; they are ever full of sap and green.*

Psalm 92:12–14 esv

"What am I going to do with my retirement?"

The anxious question came from Anne Bell, a recently retired researcher at the University of Northern Colorado. As a staff volunteer for the 5280 Fellowship, a young leaders program in Denver, Anne decided to give her first year of retirement to young professionals struggling with questions about calling. Bright and soft-spoken, wearing dark-rimmed glasses and carrying her teacher's bag, today Anne came to the office with her own questions about calling.

As our staff team discussed our weekly reading, Anne looked out on the snow-capped mountains from our seventh-story office. "What do you think, Anne?" I asked. She paused. Her voice began to quiver. "I'm really searching for what I'm called to," she confessed. "I need to know what's next."

Weeks later I visited John Beeble, a newly retired construction executive. Not wanting to fully retreat from working life, John started his own consulting company. "There's only one rule about my consulting company—no employees. I did that for twenty years," he said, with a note of weariness in his voice. Yet he violated his rule less than a year into starting his firm. As clients multiplied, he needed an executive assistant to manage the demands on his time that he thought he was leaving behind.

Less than five minutes into our conversation, John received a text from his adult daughter who asked him to babysit his grandkids, he was asked (by me) to sit on a nonprofit advisory board, and one of his clients called with an urgent need. John confessed, "I'm trying to discern what's next in this phase of life," feeling the tug between rest, family, and work. "I want to stay engaged, but not in the same way as during my career. Give me some time to figure this out."

A few days later, I struck up a conversation in my kitchen with my recently retired father-in-law, Dan Faulkner. A former city engineer, he said, "Maybe I'll give more of my time to Engineers Without Borders." But then he confessed he hadn't fully thought through his plans for retirement. He showed me pictures of a recent trip to Germany and Switzerland with his wife and dinner club friends. "Will you do more traveling in retirement?" I asked. "Yes," he replied. "But I'm not sure what I'll do back at home."

My own father, Greg, recently turned 65 and retired from a career selling print advertising. For over fourteen years, he lived in the Twin Cities while his wife, Gayle, ran Interlachen Inn, a small restaurant in Alexandria, Minnesota. Having lived apart from her for over a decade, he was ready to say good riddance to the two-hour commute every weekend, to spending nights alone, and to a life of hurry and obligation. They sold their house in Minneapolis and renovated their cabin with a deluxe fireplace, big-screen TV, and farmhouse kitchen. He was eagerly awaiting a new season of R & R.

Yet his honeymoon period was short-lived. Less than three months after retirement, my aunt Holly (his sister) went in for another round of chemotherapy, having battled cancer for years. But this time, she started to decline fast. In only weeks, he found himself coordinating hospice details, calling family, and moving her out of her apartment.

When I asked Gayle, my stepmother, about her retirement plans with my dad, she expressed excitement about having time to take road trips. Yet when the conversation turned to finances, she confessed, "We used our retirement savings to buy out our partners in the restaurant. Then over the next few years, we drained much of our savings to keep it afloat. We take a modest income from the restaurant, but finances could be on the edge at any time."

Retirement. It comes suddenly, like slamming on

the brakes after a hectic career. As I watch family and friends experience the jarring change, I've noticed that the stories they've unconsciously believed about retirement don't match their all-too-human experiences.

A glance at retirement articles online shows images of gray-haired couples walking on sandy beaches, financial gurus counseling retirees on how to stretch Social Security benefits to the max, and ads for retirement communities that promise "unlimited possibilities." (At least that's the slogan of a retirement community in Roanoke, Virginia, that promises to deliver "a lifestyle that our residents have earned and deserved.")

But beneath the propaganda, profound reservations about retirement bubble up from people like Anne, John, Dan, Greg, and Gayle.

Margaret Mark, the former head of research at the advertising agency Young & Rubicam, interviewed "retired" Americans (aged fifty-five to seventy) across all socioeconomic spectrums. In focus groups, they reported a love for their newfound freedom and a disdain for anything that sounded like punching the clock again. They lauded the glories of no longer having a commute.

Yet when asked about their overall happiness in retirement, doubts crept in. They reported a powerful sense of loneliness. Even though they had more time for family and friends, they missed the bonds they experienced at work, or "relationships with a purpose," to use Mark's words.[1]

Today there's a growing sense of uneasiness among

Americans aged 50–70. Baby boomers, and even early Gen Xers, are asking new questions about life, work, calling, and purpose in retirement—questions that our society is largely unprepared to answer.

NEW QUESTIONS FOR A NEW SOCIETY

The world is changing. An estimated eighty million baby boomers will retire in the next twenty years. At a pace of roughly 10,000 boomers retiring per day,[2] those over age 65 are the fastest-growing age demographic in the United States.[3] Wan He, Daniel Goodkind, and Paul Kowal note that it's not just the US that's getting older; the world is rapidly aging. "From 2025 to 2050 the older [over age 65] population is projected to almost double to 1.6 billion globally," they report. In 2015, only 8.5 percent of the world was over 65; by 2050, it's expected to grow to 16.7 percent.[4]

One of the causes of this population boom is that we're living longer than ever before. Lynda Gratton and Andrew Scott, authors of *The 100 Year Life: Living and Working in an Age of Longevity,* note the vast changes in life expectancy in the twentieth and now the twenty-first century. For example, if you were born in 1947, you can expect to live to age 85. If you were born in 1967, your life expectancy is 91. For those born in 2007, life expectancy is now 103.[5]

Feel like meeting a centenarian is a rarity? For children today, it will be the norm. Advances in medical technology have spawned a new age of human longevity.

As the "Graying of America" is underway, no longer are the recently retired content to sit in rocking chairs and watch their ever-expanding "golden years" pass by. Baby boomers are uneasy about outdated notions of retirement and are asking new questions about work, finances, rest, family, calling, and purpose.

Work. The dictionary defines retirement as "the action or fact of leaving one's job and ceasing to work." But many baby boomers today are rejecting the idea of completely ceasing to work for a lifetime after age 65 (or age 62, when they're first able to receive Social Security benefits). But models for what this looks like are scarce. Should baby boomers give up their jobs completely, work part-time, volunteer, or reinvent themselves for an "encore career"? What's the proper role of work in this new season of life?

Money. Finances are a major concern for most older Americans. Less than half of Americans have saved more than $10,000 for retirement and one-third have no retirement savings at all.[6] The number one financial concern among the recently retired is how to pay (or *who* pays) for rising healthcare costs as they age.[7] Add in that many state-sponsored pension systems are nearing insolvency, and the result is that millions wonder where their daily bread will come from as they age.

Time. As Americans live longer, "we do not know what we will be doing with all that time," says Joseph Coughlin, director of the Massachusetts Institute of Technology's AgeLab. Baby boomers "recognize that the current systems in place are not only inadequate to meet the demands of aging, but woefully inadequate to meet their expectations."[8] To policy-makers, long life has caused a conundrum: how should we fund pensions, Social Security, and rising healthcare costs? Yet individuals also ask questions about quality of life: is long life a gift to be enjoyed? Or instead of life being "nasty, brutish, and short," to borrow the famous phrase of seventeenth-century philosopher Thomas Hobbes, will it be nasty, brutish, and *long*?

Leisure. In retirement, how much should I travel, rest, or take up hobbies? "We live in a society driven by economics and capitalist dynamics," says Mark Galli, the 66-year-old editor in chief at *Christianity Today.* "It's all about efficiency and competitiveness. I'm looking forward to finding a more meaningful rhythm, without feeling the artificial constraints of the American economy. Perhaps I'll spend more time fly fishing."

Most older Americans want a saner schedule of work and rest in retirement. Yet a life defined only by leisure in retirement often leads to depression. The BBC reports that retirement can increase chances of clinical depression by 40 percent.[9] What, then, is the right balance between rest, work, and play?

Family. Retirement is a time for many to reassess family relationships. Caring for adult children and ailing parents, spending time with grandchildren, and reacquainting yourself with your spouse after decades on the job—retirement introduces new questions about family, friendship, independence, dependence, and multigenerational living. Questions abound: should we move closer to grandkids? How will we afford assisted living for our parents (and for ourselves one day)? How do we have a happy marriage in retirement?

Calling. "Did you have a sense of what you were called to?" I asked Tim Cunningham, a 67-year-old retired financial analyst. After reflecting on his first year of retirement, the answer was blunt: "No." He then followed up with a host of volunteer activities—sitting on the board of the weaver's guild and volunteering at the botanic gardens—sensing a void in his daily life.

For the 87 percent of baby boomers who believe in God, questions about calling often lead to questions about hearing the voice of a Caller for a new phase of life.[10] In the uncertainty of money, time, relationships, work, health, leisure, and identity, one question creeps into the prayers of baby boomers like Anne Bell: *God, do You have a purpose for my retirement?*

DECODING THE CULTURE OF RETIREMENT: FOUR POSTURES

Retirement is an idea with a history. And to understand our purpose, we first need to understand the culture surrounding retirement and the stories that shape our perceptions about work, rest, age, and meaning.

The history of retirement began in America around the idea of a never-ending *vacation.* Using that theme, here are four postures toward retirement that dominate headlines today:

1. Let's vacation.

"Wake up and live in Sun City, for an active way of life," said the radio advertising jingle for the Del Webb Corporation in 1960. "Wake up and live in Sun City, Mr. Senior Citizen and wife. Don't let retirement get you down! Be happy in Sun City; it's a paradise town." Retirement communities started appearing in the 1920s, but it was real estate developer Del Webb's Sun City, a sprawling housing development for seniors built just outside of Phoenix, Arizona, that popularized retirement as a year-round vacation in post-WWII America.

The history of retirement stretches back to 1875, when Otto von Bismarck, the minister president of Prussia, proposed government-provided financial support for citizens over the age of 70 (at a time when life expectancy was 46!). By the 1920s, several American industries, from railroads to oil to banking, provided some pensions to older Americans. In 1935 the Social Security Act passed under Franklin Delano Roosevelt, which set the retirement age initially at 65, in part to encourage older workers to exit the workforce so that younger workers affected by the Great Depression might replace them. In the 1950s, a steady expansion of benefits began—first for those in commerce and industry, and then benefits expanded to farmers, domestic workers, and the disabled. In 1965, hospital insurance arrived through the passage of Medicare.

In 1952, H. B. Kenagy of Mutual Life Insurance advised business leaders at the National Industrial Conference Board about the best way to sell retirement to their employees. He suggested distributing stories in company newsletters about happily retired people playing golf and walking on the beach. He counseled them to also emphasize "what they did to get ready for the life they are now living"[11]—like stashing a portion of their monthly salary into company pension plans. The message: *Invest now and the dream can be yours.*

The expansion of Social Security benefits and a nationwide effort to market a new "retirement lifestyle"[12] provided fertile soil for Del Webb's Sun City. On New Year's Day 1960, Webb and Tom Breen, Webb's associate, hoped for 10,000 visitors for their new creation—a housing development for seniors complete with lawn bowling, swimming pool, card rooms, auditorium, and a shopping center. Over 100,000 people arrived for the spectacle. By 1980, 50,000 people lived in Sun City, making it the seventh largest city in Arizona.

As the idyllic retirement lifestyle gained in popularity, the number of older Americans in the labor force dropped precipitously. By 1940, the first year Social Security was paid out, 41.8 percent of men over age 65 were in the labor force. By 1960, the year Sun City opened, it dropped to 30.5 percent. In 1999, it was only 16.3 percent.[13]

Today, the dominant paradigm of retirement is about *vacation*—how to afford it, and then how to make the most of it. A Google search for the word "retirement" shows articles, ads, and tips on how to save enough money for it and a host of books on how to enjoy it: *How to Retire Happy, Wild and Free, 101 Fun Things to Do in Retirement,* and *Design Your Dream Retirement.* Retirement gifts follow suit: a coffee mug that reads "Goodbye Tension, Hello Pension." A kitchen wall-hanging with the acronym R.E.T.I.R.E says *R*elax, *E*ntertain, *T*ravel, *I*ndulge, *R*ead, *E*njoy. A wine glass reads, "I can wine all I want. I'm retired."

A more whimsical version of the *Let's vacation* paradigm includes the Red Hat Society, an international women's organization for women over 50 inspired by Jenny Joseph's poem, "Warning," which begins:

> When I am an old woman I shall wear purple
> With a red hat which doesn't go, and doesn't suit
> me.[14]

I've been good long enough, goes the train of thought. Time to let loose and enjoy life. I deserve a vacation.

The problem. "I'm the guy who's got everything. I know," says Hollywood actor Brad Pitt in a *Rolling Stone* interview. "But I'm telling you, once you get everything, then you're just left with yourself. I've said it before and I'll say it again: It doesn't help you sleep any better, and you don't wake up any better because of it."[15] He could have been speaking about the dashed hopes of those expecting that a year-round vacation would satisfy their retirement dreams.

There are several problems with the *Let's vacation* paradigm. First, most Americans can't afford this vision. Second, many Christians (and people of other religions as well) believe a life of self-focused leisure doesn't square with their beliefs. And third, work might not be all that bad.

Yet the biggest reason to question the *Let's vacation* view is that it leads to boredom at minimum, and sometimes to despair. The 2015 movie *The Intern*, starring Robert De Niro, portrays a 70-year-old widower who gets bored with retirement and decides to become an intern at a tech start-up filled with millennials. People like Anne and John know from experience that the longing for purpose cannot be fulfilled through entertainment or long trips to France. Most baby boomers sense a need for rest after retirement, but they also feel the impending emptiness of the *Let's vacation* paradigm. Even lobster dinners begin to taste like soap after a while.

Rest has a role in retirement (as it does for all of life), but the *Let's vacation* view of retirement is a lot more appealing before retirement than after.

2. I can't afford to vacation.

If the dominant paradigm for retirement today is a never-ending vacation, the fastest growing group of retirees are those who know they can't afford it.

During the time I was writing this chapter, a curious gentleman who looked in his midsixties approached me while I was reading at a restaurant. "What are you reading?" he asked. "Actually," I responded, "I'm writing on retirement." He snickered, surely noticing I'm some years away from retirement and perhaps reflecting on his own experience. I asked, "Do you happen to know something about retirement?" Without a pause, he replied, "Yep. Not enough money."

He's not alone. The economic problems facing most

Americans at retirement are mounting. The Center for Retirement Research at Boston College estimates that 52 percent of Americans may not be able to maintain their standard of living in retirement, which it defines as an income not more than 10 percent below the replacement rate (65–85 percent of their previous income). To make that concrete, the average retirement assets of those aged 50–59 in 2013 were just $110,000, yet they need $250,000 just to generate $10,000 in annual income.

But there's still Social Security to supplement savings, right? On current projections, Social Security reserves will run out by 2034.[16] Though claims that Social Security payments will go to $0 are overblown, if no changes are made, benefits will have to be reduced by 20 percent, according to the 2017 annual report of the trust fund's Board of Trustees.[17]

Recently our church's children's ministry performed a Christmas pageant at a low-income retirement apartment complex in Colorado. As I walked to the community room, the hallways were dim, a musty smell filled the air, and I could hear doors lock as I passed by the apartments. Jean, a kind volunteer who lives there, said to me, "My son says this place should be torn down as a slum." She chuckled. I got worried. Here is the opposite side of the *Let's vacation* paradigm, I thought. Today there are an estimated 25 million Americans over age 60 who experience "economic insecurity."

If the great American dream is "financial freedom" in a blissful retirement, the great American frustration is that such a dream is out of reach for the majority.

A mix of factors is creating a perfect storm for baby boomers entering retirement:

- Baby boomers are one of the largest generations in American history.
- A growing number of Americans struggle financially during their working life and struggle to save enough for retirement in the first place.
- Pension plans—from corporations to state governments—are underfunded, and some (like the state of Illinois) are facing unprecedented challenges.[18]
- Healthcare costs are rising.
- Americans are living longer than ever, often outstripping their savings.

Forbes reports that Europe isn't faring much better. From the UK to Italy to Greece to Spain, pension debt as a percentage of GDP is on the rise.[19]

Not exactly encouraging news.

Mitch Anthony, author of *The New Retirementality* writes, "Retirement is an illusion because those who can afford the illusion are disillusioned by it, and those who cannot afford the illusion are haunted by it."[20]

The problem. The unfulfilled promise of "Sun City for all" is causing mounting resentment among working-class citizens. The challenge for millions is practical: How will I pay my bills for the next ten, twenty, or thirty years? Will I have to work until I'm 70? Or 80? Will I be forced into government-subsidized housing or become a burden on my children?

These questions are not easily addressed. Policy-makers are sweating to figure out what many are calling a "retirement crisis."

Yet many boomers recognize that "having it all" won't necessarily lead to a purposeful retirement, either. They're actively seeking ways to cut costs and find meaning apart from money. New questions arise: Are there pathways for contentment that money cannot bring? Might I still work into my seventies or even eighties—and still enjoy life? Considering how much money I have, what *can* I do to live fully right now?

3. A never-ending vacation isn't biblical.

"Lord, spare me this curse [of retirement]!"[21] says John Piper, the former pastor of Bethlehem Baptist in Minneapolis and bestselling author. Piper calls his flock to "resolutely resist retirement" and "spend ourselves in the sacrifices of love, not the accumulation of comforts."[22] Ralph Winter, founder of the U.S. Center for World Mission, echoes Piper's sentiment: "Most men don't die of old age, they die of retirement. . . . Where in the Bible do they see [retirement]? Did Moses retire? Did Paul retire? Peter? John? Do military officers retire in the middle of a war?"[23]

A handful of Christian leaders point out that retirement is "unbiblical" (which, of course, is true since retirement is a recent idea). The closest the Bible comes to our modern idea of retirement is found Numbers 8:25: "And from the age of fifty years they [the Levites] shall withdraw from the duty of the service and serve no more" (ESV). Since hauling around the furniture for the tabernacle was hard physical labor, older Levites were commanded to "minister to their brothers in the tent of meeting"—a hint that God doesn't intend for our work to completely stop, but instead to morph and mature with age.

The problem. The main problem with this "resist retirement" view is that most people cannot imagine working, nonstop, for forty, fifty, or even sixty years. And for good reason. Work is often painful—mind-numbing tasks, humiliating bosses, a lack of autonomy, crammed schedules, coworker conflict, physical exhaustion, new technology, oppressive hours. William Faulkner once wrote, "You can't eat for eight hours a day nor drink for eight hours a day nor make love for eight hours a day—all you can do for eight hours is work. Which is the reason why man makes himself and everybody else so miserable." Perhaps this is overstating the case, but the author of Ecclesiastes joins in: "So I hated life, because the work that is done under the sun was grievous to me. All of it is meaningless, a chasing after the wind" (2:17).

Many leading Christian voices rightly point out that we never retire from our vocations (see chapter 3), but they overlook the suffering, the thorns and thistles, and the pain that so many people experience on this side of Eden (Gen. 3:17–19).

Retirement as a never-ending vacation may indeed be less than God's intent for His people, but so is an exhausted soul. A Christian perspective on retirement needs more than "never retire, keep working." It needs a restoration of work, rest, and service that matures over a lifetime.

COMMON:
One Christian perspective on retirement: never retire, keep working.

vs.

UNCOMMON:
Restore a balance of work, rest, and service that matures over a lifetime.

Retirement may be just the opportunity to reassess these foundations of a fruitful life.

4. Vacationing isn't as satisfying as world changing.

Quickly establishing itself as an alternative to the *Let's vacation* paradigm is a widespread movement toward "encore careers." Led by the talented Marc Freedman, author of books like *Encore: Finding Work That Matters in the Second Half of Life* and *Prime Time: How Baby Boomers Will Revolutionize Retirement and Transform America,* the story about retirement is shifting away from leisure toward social entrepreneurship and civic engagement.

For Freedman, baby boomers are not a liability but instead an opportunity to address the great social challenges of our day. "Our enormous and rapidly growing older population—commonly portrayed as a burden to the nation and a drain on future generations—is a vast, untapped social resource," writes Freedman. "If we can engage these individuals in ways that fill urgent gaps in our society, the result would be a windfall for American civic life in the twenty-first century."[24]

Countries like Germany, who also have a rapidly aging population, are realizing that more seniors want to rejoin the workforce. Companies like car maker Daimler and retailer Otto are trying to regain skilled labor from retirees intent on making a contribution.[25]

Other voices have followed suit, calling for "unretirement" and renewed social engagement that spurns a life of leisured self-focus in favor of joining the Peace Corps, reinventing yourself in a new career field, or volunteering with troubled youth.

If purpose was elusive during your career, the thinking goes, perhaps now is the time to find it through civic service.

The problem. There's lots to praise about the Encore Movement. It swaps a vision of consumption for service, of acquiring for giving. Serving at Volunteers in Medicine (VIM) Clinics or taking a trip with Elderhostel (a nonprofit that provides educational opportunities for adults over 55) is a recipe for more fulfillment than another 18 holes of golf.

Moreover, leaders like Freedman have done us a favor in pointing out the obvious: Today, we tell productive, able, bright citizens in their sixties to stop working in what's often the prime of their career, and start collecting a pension . . . sometimes for decades. This is not only expensive, it's also misaligned with a boomer generation that's more interested in meaningful contribution than living in a Caribbean cruise commercial.

But there are three weaknesses to this movement. First, it often overlooks the realities of aging. Backs ache. Bodies change. Funerals become a regularity. Time changes us all. As one woman told me, "Purpose must go deeper than world-changing. I'm not a solution to a social problem. I'm a person. I have energy, for sure. But I'm not a millennial and don't want to be." The place of human weakness and frailty (at any age) often gets lost in accounts of civic heroism.

Second, baby boomers are human, which means they are beautiful yet flawed. Saying that the boomer generation is a great solution to our social ills belies what we know about ourselves. We're deposed royalty, says Blaise Pascal, and when we're honest, we're drawn to greed as much as generosity, sloth as much as diligence, cowardice as much as courage.[26]

Movements like Encore are framed by a humanistic story, which is especially prominent in the tech start-up world, but also among entrepreneurs and policy-makers. And the story is pretty simple. *There is no problem that human beings can't fix.* But the reason I know this story isn't true is that I can't even fix myself. (My wife knows this full well.) An accurate story for retirement needs the drama of both sin and grace. It needs to acknowledge we can't solve the essential problem of sin, both individually and societally. We need a solution from outside ourselves.

The third problem with these movements as a story for retirement has to do with the human longing for purpose. Over a generation ago, Bob Buford wrote the bestselling book *Halftime,* which coined the phrase "from success to significance." I asked Fred Smith, the founder of The Gathering, an annual conference for Christian philanthropists, what he thought about the idea of significance. "It's like drinking salt water," he said. "Looking for significance from external things is still competing for somebody else's 'OK.' It just leaves you thirsty."

The *motivation* behind our service is critical. If it's merely to solve social issues, we will always find more issues to solve and feel like we have never done enough. Ironically, the same exhausting treadmill from our careers can follow us into "more meaningful" work.

Ethel Percy Andrus, the founder of the American Association of Retired Persons (now just AARP) established the organization's motto as "To Serve, Not to Be Served." If we listen carefully, in one of the world's largest nonprofit organizations we can still hear the echoes of one who gave "his life as a ransom for many."

Retirement needs a new story. Or better yet, a very old story.

THE SCENT OF RESURRECTION

Gary VanderArk is a not-so-retired neurosurgeon living in south Denver. In his late 70s, he continues to teach five classes of medical students at the University of Colorado

Anschutz Medical Center, serve on nearly a dozen non-profit boards, and bike almost twenty miles a day. Gary was also the founder of Doctors Care, a nonprofit that has helped thousands of Colorado's medically underserved. If anybody has a "right" to hang up his cleats and slow down, it's Gary. Yet when I interviewed him about what motivates him, he said with a broad grin, "Well, I believe it's more blessed to give than to receive. I'm enjoying myself too much to stop."

With his white hair, slender fingers, and frail voice, to some Gary may seem "old." But when you speak with him, he seems almost carefree, like a child on Christmas morning. He acknowledges human frailty and death, yet keeps serving others as if death is of no concern to him. He keeps teaching and sitting on non-profit boards not because of social duty, but instead out of sheer delight. He is quick to listen and slow to speak. His words hold genuine gravitas. He is like "the righteous [who] flourish like the palm tree and grow like a cedar in Lebanon . . . They still bear fruit in old age; they are ever full of sap and green" (Ps. 92:12–14 ESV).

George MacDonald once wrote, "Age is not all decay. It is the ripening, the swelling of the fresh life within that withers and bursts the husk." This is Gary.

Gary, like many of God's people through the ages, lives a story that culminates on Sunday morning. It is the first day of the week. It's the dawn of a new world.

"What am I going to do with my retirement?" asks Anne Bell and a generation of baby boomers entering into a new phase of life.

To answer that question, the first thing to do after retirement is not to travel, volunteer, or find a new career. To find a pathway to the vibrancy of a Gary VanderArk, what's most needed after a lifetime of work (and often toil) is to first take a season of deep Sabbath rest.

Chapter 2

Sabbath

*"Come to me, all you who are weary
and burdened, and I will give you rest."*

Matthew 11:28

"I'd done all the preparation, except to really think about what life was going to be like," said Sue Ellen King, who had worked as a care nurse and nursing educator at the University of Florida Health for thirty-eight years. According to a *New York Times* article about "unretirement," after King retired, she organized photos and had long lunches with friends but found herself feeling adrift after only three months. The weeklong trip to Hilton Head, South Carolina, was enjoyable, but the satisfaction was fleeting.

Similarly, Michelle Wallace, who lives in Broomfield, Colorado, had a frustrating twenty months after she retired from a high-stress job in telecommunications. "I felt like I was free-floating, bobbing along on the ocean," she said. "I felt very ungrounded." Her friends noticed her mood swings; doctors began pre-scribing anti-depressants.[1]

Today baby boomers and many Gen Xers are questioning whether a vacation attitude toward retirement can answer questions about purpose, identity, and deep rest after thirty or even forty years without more than two weeks off annually.

Retirees need more than a vacation or a premature jump back into the workforce. Instead, the early years of retirement provide the perfect time to take a much-needed sabbatical.

RESTING FROM VACATION

"Retirement? That is an ongoing relentless effort in creativity," says Ben Whittaker, the lead character in Nancy Meyers's film *The Intern*. "Golf, books, movies, pinochle. Tried yoga, learned to cook, bought some plants, took classes in Mandarin. 相信我。我已经尝试了一切。Translation: Believe me, I've tried everything."[2]

Ben recounts his retirement experience on a video recording, applying for an internship at a tech company as a 70-year-old widower:

> At first, I admit, I sort of enjoyed the novelty of it. It felt like I was playing hooky. I used all the miles I'd saved and traveled the globe. The problem was, no matter where I went, as soon as I got home, the "nowhere to-be" thing hit me like a ton of bricks. . . . Don't get me wrong, I'm not an unhappy person. Quite the

contrary. I just know there's a hole in my life, and I
need to fill it. Soon.[3]

Meyers, a boomer herself, expresses the tension of
retirement in a two minute and ten second opening
monologue (she both wrote and produced the movie).
Retirement as a life of vacation has an initial appeal, but
eventually it leaves many with a sense of needing to fill
a "hole in my life."

After a lifetime of work, the first instinct of retirement is to take a vacation. Whether that involves
house projects or trips to Holland, the instinct to *rest* is
understandable.

But for many, vacations, like the first year of retirement, often leave retirees feeling *restless*, not rested.
The absence of work commitments is back-filled with
television watching, playing online games, shopping,
or harried household projects. Life can feel like a messy
garage: disorganized and cluttered with leftovers from
a too-busy career. Internally, something inside us keeps
working—even on vacation.

The word *vacation* derives from the Latin *vacare*,
from which we get "to vacate, make empty, make
void." That's an accurate word for how many view time
off. We seek to *vacate* our lives for a few days or weeks,
whether on the beaches of Mexico or in the mountains
of Colorado. Vacation is fun—for a week or two. But
vacation as an ongoing lifestyle is often an attempt to
escape from reality.

Whether we make work the source of our identity

or empty work of any meaning past a paycheck, many newly retired people say: *Enough. I'm done. Time to finally spend time on "me."*

Mary is a 60-year-old woman. One day, she heard Marc Freedman, the founder of Civic Ventures, waxing eloquent about the civic heroism of older Americans on National Public Radio. She called in and said bluntly, "I would like to disagree with everything that's been said." Freedman was stunned. How could anyone disagree with the idea that older adults are a social asset to our communities? She told her story: she landed her first job as a teenager. After raising two kids and working for forty years straight, she finally grew tired of her boss heaping on more and more work. At the first opportunity she got, she retired.[4]

Mary, like many others, entered into retirement longing for rest and renewal. But vacation isn't the answer. *The answer is to begin retirement with a stretch of deep Sabbath rest.*

THE REASON FOR SABBATH

On the dusty sands of the Sinai desert, Moses descended from the mountain with a message from God. "Remember the Sabbath day by keeping it holy. Six days you shall labor and do all your work, but the seventh day is a Sabbath to the LORD your God" (Ex. 20:8–10).

Why include a day of rest among the Ten Commandments upon which He would build a new society? And why should we consider Sabbath rest—or a season of "sabbatical rest" — as a better category for early retirement than vacation? The Old Testament suggests three reasons.

Trust

"For in six days the LORD made the heavens and the earth, the sea, and all that is in them, but he rested on the seventh day" (Ex. 20:11). Moses gives the Israelites the reason for Sabbath: God Himself rested after six days of work in creating the world. There's a pattern, woven into the fabric of the universe by the Creator. It's like gravity or the laws of motion. To be like God — and to become fully human — we need both work and rest in proper proportion.

> ## COMMON:
> ### After a lifetime of work, the first instinct of retirement is to take a vacation.
> ### vs.
> ## UNCOMMON:
> ### To be like God—and to become fully human—we need both work and rest in proper proportion.

Sabbath reminds us to recognize our proper role in the cosmos. Biblical scholar Craig Slane says, "In ceasing from labor one is reminded of one's true status as a dependent being, of the God who cares for and sustains all his creatures, and of the world as a reality belonging ultimately to God."[5] Like children dependent upon their parents, Sabbath makes us see that food, clothes, sunlight, friendship, air—all are gifts from the Creator, not mere products of our labor. The Bible continually points to God as the ultimate provider.

But we have surely worked for and paid for all those "gifts," right? God does give people the gift of working as colaborers in His ongoing creation and cultivation of the earth (Gen. 1:27–28; 2:15). But we are not all-powerful. In Sabbath, God says, "Enjoy your work, but think not of yourself as masters of the universe. That is my role."

ING, a financial services company, aired a series of commercials in 2008 centered on the idea of "What's your number?" That is, how much money do you need to retire? A man bikes with the number $1,269,407 under his arm. A woman walks into an office, carrying the number $675,423 as if it were a purse. A man sits in a clinic with his pregnant wife, holding "his" number. The idea is that once we have saved a certain amount of money, we will have the ability to "retire in comfort." Here is where our security lies.

Saving money for future needs is wise (Prov. 10:4-5). But the Bible suggests trusting in "our number" as a blanket of assurance is idolatry—the worship of a false god.

Jesus tells the story of a man who built two barns as a hedge against insecurity. The wealthy man says to himself, "'You have plenty of grain laid up for many years. Take life easy; eat, drink and be merry.' But God said to him, 'You fool! This very night your life will be demanded from you. Then who will get what you have prepared for yourself?'" (Luke 12:19–20).

Sabbath reframes retirement debates about money, retirement, and security. Whether clothed in gold like Solomon or in rags like Lazarus, Sabbath calls us to *trust God to provide for our needs.* Taking a sabbatical can release the chains of anxiety and restore us to our proper place as created beings, dependent on God the Father for every good gift (James 1:17).

Identity

"Remember that you were slaves in Egypt," says Deuteronomy's version of the fourth commandment, "and that the Lᴏʀᴅ your God brought you out of there with a mighty hand and an outstretched arm" (5:15). Why not work every day of the week? Only slaves do that, suggests the Bible. God is the one who has redeemed His people from slavery, and Sabbath was to be a continual reminder of their liberty and identity as God's people.

In 2018, Americans left a total of 705 million vacation days unused.[6] *Project Time Off* reports that 61 percent feared looking replaceable at work, and 56 percent said "nobody else could do my job."[7] Why the nonstop work? I believe America's work-a-holism flows from a question of identity. If we're not our jobs, then who are we? What is our real value?

Centuries ago, the Israelites were called to *remember the Sabbath* as a reminder that their value was not derived from their work. The practice of Sabbath was a call to re-center their collective identity on God's vision for them as a people. The Israelites were God's treasured possession, a royal priesthood, and a holy nation (Ex. 19:5; cf. 1 Peter 2:9).

Work was created to be an expression of our identity, not the source of our identity.

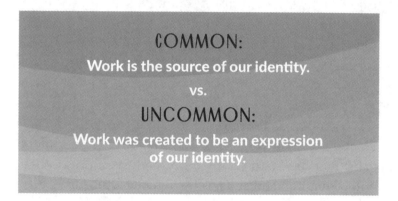

COMMON:
Work is the source of our identity.

vs.

UNCOMMON:
Work was created to be an expression of our identity.

One of the "thorns and thistles" of retirement is that it reveals where we've put our identity too fully in our careers. The report isn't due, the phone stops ringing, and it feels like nobody needs you anymore. The recently retired often feel a sense of loss and separation.

But this pain, argues Gordon Smith, author and president of Ambrose University in Calgary, can be transfigured into a deepening sense of vocation and contribution.

I am convinced that part of the essence of vocational identity during this period of our lives [the senior years] is that we let go of power and control: people listen to us because we are wise and because we bless, not because of our office or any formal structure of power.[8]

Sabbath calls us to root our identity in God's action on our behalf and let go of an identity that was too wrapped up in our jobs. (We'll return to the theme of identity and calling in the next chapter.) Taking a sabbatical can heal past wounds as we re-center our identity on being God's sons and daughters.

Justice

The command to observe the Sabbath includes a command to allow those with the least cultural power (children, servants, foreigners) to rest so that they "may be refreshed" (Ex. 23:12). "On it [the Sabbath] you shall not do any work, neither you, nor your son or daughter, nor your male or female servant, nor your animals, nor any foreigner residing in your towns" (20:10). The Bible continually connects the observance of Sabbath with justice.

My friend Josué Franco is a greeter at Walmart. As an immigrant from South America now pushing 75 years old (he's never been able to afford "retirement"), he recently shared with me about why he often must miss church on Sundays. "I always get scheduled on the weekends. And what can I do? I have to work—but I miss being here," he said, almost crestfallen. "I'm sorry, Jeff."

For Josué, Sunday is not just the chance to worship, it's a time to be with family and friends. When he must work while others shop, his opportunities for meaningful relationships diminish.

Josué's story clarified something for me. Sabbath is not just about individual spiritual practice. It's also about making space for the restoration *of others*. There are two explicit prohibitions in the law regarding Sabbath: no fires were to be kindled in Jewish dwellings (Ex. 35:3), and no one was to leave their place (16:29). That is, not only were they to cease from productivity (fires were used for everything from cooking to making tools), but they were not to engage in commerce, forcing others to work on the Sabbath.

The prophets regularly connect Sabbath observance to a just society (Isa. 58:6–8, 13). Not only does round-the-clock work oppress the powerless, it suggests *idolatry*. Sabbath observance was an outward sign of whether people were keeping the first and most important commandment, "You shall have no other gods before me" (Ex. 20:3).

Vacations tend to prioritize our own luxury, consumption, and comfort; Sabbath sets limits for our work in order to create economic, social, and spiritual renewal for all social classes.

Historian Paul Johnson writes about the Sabbath, "The day of rest is one of the great Jewish contributions to the comfort and joy of mankind."[9] Perhaps taking a post-career sabbatical could also be a great contribution to the contemporary experience of retirement.

PLANNING A SABBATICAL

What if we decided that the early years of retirement were the best time to take a true sabbatical? What might six months, nine months, or even a full year of deep, Sabbath rest look like?[10] How might we spend time in order to expand and redirect our sense of vocation for the next season of life (the topic of the next chapter)?

My argument is that sabbatical is a way to structure time in early retirement to heal past wounds, seek God's voice, and find God's call for the next season of life.

Does this, then, mean a year of twiddling your thumbs? Not at all. Though many put boundaries around technology use, economic consumption, and work activities on their Sabbath days, Sabbath is not only about what not to do.

Here are nine practices to consider as you plan your sabbatical:

Prepare

The Jewish Day of Preparation was a weekly rhythm of preparing to rest well—and it required extra work. Jews would store food and goods so they wouldn't need to purchase them on the Sabbath day. They informed Gentiles (non-Jews) of their intention to take Sabbath rest.

Sabbaticals must be intentionally prepared for rather than stumbled into.

Consider taking two or three weeks to consider how you will restructure your time in sabbatical. What responsibilities can you hand off before you begin? What will your days, weeks, and months look like? And most importantly, who will journey with you into sabbatical? Judith Shulevitz's *Then Sabbath World: Glimpses of a Different Order of Time* notes that Sabbath is a *communal*, not individualistic, activity.[11] Consider doing a sabbatical with a friend or spouse and making plans in a trusted community.

Feast

The idea of Sabbath as dour law-keeping is from the Pharisees of Jesus' day, not from God. In Jewish tradition, Sabbath was a time for richly eating and drinking. It was one of the "festivals of the LORD" that prohibited fasting and outward expressions of mourning (Lev. 23). Sabbath was to be a "delight," recounting God's grace toward His people (Isa. 58:13).

On your sabbatical, consider having a lavish feast— or several—for former coworkers, family, and friends as a way to look back on a career with gratitude. You could do this once a month or once a quarter. In Israel, feast days were markers of time. Joyful celebration can also form the chronological foundation of your sabbatical year.

Worship

In Lauren Winner's book *Mudhouse Sabbath*, she notes the difference between contemporary visions of a day of rest and the biblical vision of Sabbath. "Whom is the contemporary Sabbath designed to honor?" she asks, tongue in cheek. "Whom does it benefit? Why, the bubble-bath taker herself, of course!"[12] In contrast, Winner says, in the Bible the seventh day is a Sabbath *to the Lord your God*. The difference between "indulge, you deserve it" (the popular vision for retirement) and "drink in the joy of God" could not be starker.

As you plan your sabbatical year, leave time for communal worship, for long and short periods of silence, for prayer walks, and for studying Scripture. Worship is the center of Sabbath.

Re-create

Sports, hobbies, music, theater—these all can play an important role in a sabbatical year. Jewish *culture* was built around its festivals and celebrations. Recreation as "re-creation," rather than leisure or vacation, can be an ingredient in renewal.

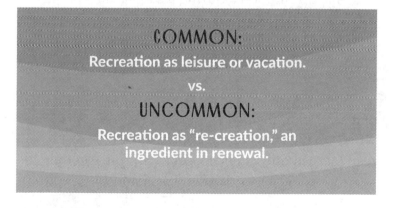

COMMON:
Recreation as leisure or vacation.

vs.

UNCOMMON:
Recreation as "re-creation," an ingredient in renewal.

But might recreation be turned into a kind of work, a way to "occupy my time" in retirement? Leisure can lead to a busied pattern of entertainment, rather than space to rest, reflect, and heal. Even vacation can be turned into a frantic pace of busied work.

What is the difference between work and non-work? Wouldn't woodworking be work to a carpenter, but a hobby for a banker? Or could Sudoku puzzles be work to a math teacher, but just plain fun for a retired electrician?

The key, I believe, is not to make an extrabiblical set of rules about what counts as work and what doesn't on a sabbatical (Jewish and Christian history is filled with such failed experiments). The key is to pay attention to the internal dialogue of your heart, even during recreational activities.

The Benedictine monks practiced *ora et labora* (pray and work). They endeavored to be aware of God's presence while farming, working, or even doing dishes. Can you take up carpentry during a sabbatical, yet quietly listen to God's voice? Or internally are you "cranking work out"? The difference between the two heart attitudes is the difference between work and rest, Sabbath keeping and Sabbath breaking.

Audrey Assad and Isaac Wardell, singer-songwriters of the vocation-themed album *Porter's Gate: Work Songs*, write, "In the fields of the Lord, our work is rest." Recreational activities, done in a spirit of rest, can train the heart to reengage work after a sabbatical in a spirit of peace.

Remember

Take time to write down the good gifts God has given over a lifetime of work. Get out picture albums, invite over old friends for coffee, and *remember*. Remembering was a core Sabbath practice for the Israelites. Even amid the pain of unfaithful kings, the breach of covenant, and eventual exile, they found new life in remembering the Exodus and their nation's birth out of slavery.

Ann Voskamp's *One Thousand Gifts: Dare to Live Fully Right Where You Are* is a beautiful book that portrays her odyssey of actually writing down and noticing commonplace and everyday gifts. Experiment with this during your sabbatical. Notice God's gifts— the smell of warm bread, a phone call from your daughter, the way afternoon light sparkles through the kitchen window. Remember. Be filled with gratitude.

Love your neighbor

"It is lawful to do good on the Sabbath," Jesus said as the crippled man "stretched [his hand] out, and it was restored" (Matt. 12:9–12 ESV). The Pharisees saw this and conspired to kill Him, calling Him a law breaker. But Jesus saw that Sabbath was for the restoration of all His people, especially the poor, widows, orphans, and foreigners.

During your sabbatical year, consider visiting shut-ins, sitting with tearful friends who've lost loved ones, or praying with pregnant teens at a local clinic. Bob Cutillo, a physician at the Colorado Coalition for the Homeless, once told me, "Don't serve the poor. *See through the eyes of the poor.*"

Sabbatical is a space in time for seeing what you otherwise were too busy or distracted to see during your career.

Also, beware of partaking in heroism during your sabbatical. It's likely that caring for the needs of the poor will be a far greater gift to you than it is to them.

Practice simplicity

"'Tis a gift to be simple, 'tis a gift to be free." The classic Quaker song offers a countercultural freedom from the entertainment and accumulation-complex of retirement: to possess *less* and intentionally simplify your life is to experience deep freedom.

A common early-retirement practice is to declutter—garages, storage bins, closets. Many also transition to smaller homes. Yet the Christian practice of simplicity adds a layer of spiritual restoration. "Throughout church history followers of Jesus have intentionally vowed to live simply," says author Adele Calhoun. "Following the example of the Lord, they have given up comfort and possessions and the clutter of life to leave larger spaces for loving God and neighbor. Simplicity creates margins and spaces and openness in our lives."[13]

In sabbatical, develop the habit of giving things away. Reject things that are causing anxiety in you. Learn to enjoy things without owning them.[14]

Renew your mind

"One of the people who most impressed me during my research," said Michael Lindsay, the president of Gordon College, "was John Mendelsohn." As I interviewed Michael about his book *View From the Top*, he shared about an infectious learner, Dr. Mendelsohn, who used to be the head of the prestigious M. D. Anderson Cancer Center in Houston.

"When I was doing the interview," Michael remembered, "he was reading a book on the history of opera."[15] What does the history of opera have to do with cancer research? I thought. Nothing. And that was Michael's point about learning and long-lasting contribution: people with deep, long-lasting influence cultivate a "liberal arts mentality," in which they learn far outside of their field. Such a broadening education allows them to innovate across disciplines, understand society broadly, and influence larger cultural conversations with wisdom (one of the traditional roles of an elder in the Bible).

During sabbatical, consider taking time to "be transformed by the renewing of your mind" (Rom. 12:1–2). Read not only religious books, but anything from neuroscience to wildlife biology to the history of water rights in the West. Our careers have a way of making us technicians—we know everything about one topic, but remain in the dark about most of the world. We'll return to this in chapter 7, but reigniting your curiosity and sense of wonder is crucial to cultivating wisdom, a virtue the world needs from baby boomers in the next generation.

Decide when your sabbatical will end

As we'll explore in chapter 4, we're created to work, and sabbaticals (like Sabbath days) are meant to end. "Six days you *shall labor and do all your work*," says the commandment, and that commandment is applicable over a lifetime, even as varieties of work may change (Ex. 20:9). Sabbatical is also a critical time for reevaluating your sense of calling. But setting a defined period of time—whether that be three months, six months, or a full year—focuses a sabbatical, prevents it from melting into a never-ending vacation, and instead prepares the heart to listen to God's voice for next steps.

I was once preaching on the topic of work and rest when a (very) elderly man came to me and said, "Son, I'm 91 years old. Don't you think I should be able to take a break at my age?" I muttered an embarrassed, "Yes, sir," as I was only in my early thirties at the time. He continued, "But let me tell you something. I'm a retired professor at Moody Bible Institute. I love writing but haven't done any writing for years. I'm going to take up writing again tomorrow morning."

He paused, then looked me in the eye. "Thank you, son."

A COLORFUL SYMPHONY

In Norton Juster's classic children's book *The Phantom Tollbooth*, Milo, the main character, meets Chroma the Great, "conductor of color, maestro of pigment, and director of the entire spectrum." Milo learns that Chroma is the conductor of a great symphony—piccolos, flutes, clarinets, oboes, bassoons, horns, trumpets, and tubas, which causes the sun to rise each day and shed color on nature. Every evening as Chroma lifts his arms, his symphony plays and a dash of color fills the sky. "What pleasure to lead my violins in a serenade of spring green," Chroma says, "or hear my trumpets blare out the blue sea and then watch the oboes tint it all in warm yellow sunshine."

One day, Milo wonders what it would be like if he tried to lead the orchestra himself. He raises his hands before dawn and a piccolo sends a sprite of yellow in the sky. With another movement of his arms, the cellos make the hills glow red. But then things start to go wrong. As his untrained arms flail, the sun goes up and down and up again, green snow begins to fall, and the flowers turn black. A week passes by in only four minutes. All the colors are now wrong, and Milo says unhappily, "I wish I hadn't started."[16]

The instinct in our working lives is to try to conduct the symphony by ourselves. And when things go wrong (as they always do), the instinct is to regain control in retirement by waving our arms and trying to summon satisfaction from fleeting pleasure, deep rest from vacation, or by immediately going into another field of work, hoping it will finally satisfy the longings of the heart.

But this is the countercultural wisdom of Christian faith for retirement. Sabbath rest allows us to pause and see the great, colorful symphony that is God's world.

A sabbatical structures time so we can develop the spiritual muscles to hear the voice of God, see the beauty of creation, and embrace our place in it.

"What am I going to do with my retirement?" Anne asked me not so long ago. The still, quiet whisper of the Conductor calls us, I believe, first to take a season of deep, Sabbath rest. Sabbatical is the time to ask the honest question, "God, what are You calling me to do in retirement?"

Chapter 3

Calling

*"'Love the Lord your God with all your heart
and with all your soul and with all your mind
and with all your strength.' The second is this:
'Love your neighbor as yourself.' There is no
commandment greater than these."*

Mark 12:30–31

"Linda and I decided to take a purposeful pause to listen for God's voice." In 2006, Barry Rowan was the CFO of Nextel Partners, a wireless phone company. After years of high-pressure positions, Rowan decided to take a sabbatical. He took silent retreats, mentored younger business leaders in Seattle, and spent up to two hours a day "just sitting with the Lord." During his sabbatical, he spoke with many of his friends to discern next steps for his life.

Scratched in a personal journal entry under the title "New Wine, New Wineskins," he asked a new set of questions to discern God's call: "What would it be like to go back out into the world in a new way? How would I behave differently? What things would be deepened in me?" He remembers, "I left my time off with a deeper level of surrender and a deeper appreciation that I had become less, and God had become more in me."[1]

Sabbatical structures time to allow us to hear the voice of God. *Listening to God's voice is at the heart of discerning your calling.* The word vocation comes from the Latin root *vox,* meaning voice. (I use the word vocation and calling synonymously in this book.) Vocation was originally about responding to the voice of God in all areas of life.

Kate Harris, the former executive director of the Washington Institute for Faith, Vocation & Culture, points out that in today's culture, the word vocation has been twisted from its original meaning.[2] Instead, for many it refers to an ideal job, one that forever seems over the rainbow. For others, it means becoming a pastor or priest. The original concept has been buried under dusty layers of career counseling, psychology, and a culture enamored with individual success and personal fulfillment.

To recover the gem of vocation—and what it means for a purpose-filled retirement—the concept of calling first requires some myth-busting.

SAVING THE CONCEPT OF CALLING

Four myths surround our current understanding of calling.

My calling is to do what I love.

We've said it for so long to both graduating college students and now retiring men and women that it's become almost gospel. "Do what you're passionate about. Follow your dreams. Do what you love and you'll never work another day in your life." But is this wisdom or just hot air?

By "vocation," Christians have rarely if ever meant "do what you love." More often than not, the call of God was actually a call to suffer for the sake of others. Moses was called from the desert to free the Israelites from slavery, only to be given the task of wandering the desert for forty years with a bunch of grumblers. Jeremiah was called to suffer as a prophet to the nations, a calling he rued later in his life. ("Cursed be the day I was born! May the day my mother bore me not be blessed!" Jer. 20:14.) Paul was called to be the great apostle to the Gentiles, and God tells him through Ananias, "I will show him how much he must suffer for my name" (Acts 9:16). These "callings" are not exactly "do what you love."[3]

The biblical view of calling speaks to a much deeper satisfaction of following God in every circumstance, come what may.

Calling means getting my ideal job.

Gordon Marino, a professor at St. Olaf College in Northfield, Minnesota, wrote an op-ed for the *New York Times* recounting stories of college students "rubbing their hands together, furrowing their brows" wondering if they should become doctors, philosophers, or stand-up comics. Yet many people in Northfield, he noticed, get up each day and lay roofing tiles or deliver news-papers, and worry very little about "do what you love." His dad was one of them.[4] (So was mine.) The rub is that the "ideal job" ethos is actually elitist because it under-mines work that is not done out of "passion."[5] In my view, it also can devolve into being overly self-focused. And it can cloud our vision for the redemptive nature of suffering, even inside of our callings.

The vast majority of seminars on calling in retire-ment follow this do-what-you-love paradigm. Not only is this view in tension with the call to "take up [your] cross and follow me" (Matt. 16:24), it assumes the time and money to choose among many good options—a choice millions of Americans entering retirement with minimal financial resources don't have.

I do believe there can be greater convergence of gift-ing and service in retirement, but calling first needs to be saved from a narrative about a satisfactory private life. The road to deep freedom in retirement is found not in self-actualization, but in self-surrender.

A calling is a life-stage.

More recently in conversations about retirement, "calling" has been used to denote a life-stage. "First calling" is youth and education, "second calling" is career, and "third calling" is retirement.

There are two issues with this. First, there's really no biblical support for dividing life neatly into three

> ## COMMON:
> ### The road to deep freedom in retirement is found in self-actualization.
>
> ### vs.
>
> ## UNCOMMON:
> ### The road to deep freedom in retirement is found in self-surrender.

chapters, each representing a distinctive "calling." Yet there's a bigger issue: the entire idea of a "three chapter" life needs challenging. In an age of human longevity, lives, relationships, and work and rest will become far more fluid. (We'll return to this theme in chapter 5.)

Conversations about calling are just for 20 year olds.

It can be disorienting to re-evaluate a sense of calling in your sixties, but it's also very normal. I've found through my work at Denver Institute for Faith & Work that it's the second most common time people ask deeper questions about purpose, job choice, and meaning.

Author Os Guinness writes eloquently about the life-long nature of discerning your calling. "In many cases a clear sense of calling comes only through a time of searching, including trial and error. And what may be clear to us in our twenties may be far more mysterious in our fifties because God's complete designs for us are never fully understood, let alone fulfilled, in this life."[6]

Though that may be true, age can give in fact a *deepening* sense of God's call. Here's how Jayber Crow, the lead character of Wendell Berry's classic novel, looks back on his own life as a barber:

> . . . I know I've been lucky. Beyond that, the question is if I have not been also blessed, as I believe I have—and, beyond that, even called. Surely I was called to be, for one thing, a barber . . . in spite of my intentions to the contrary.
>
> Now I have had most of the life I am going to have, and I can see what it has been. I can remember those early years when it seemed to me I was cut completely adrift, and times when, looking back at earlier times, it seemed I had been wandering in the dark woods of error. *But now it looks to me as though I was following a path that was laid out for me, unbroken, and maybe even as straight as possible, from one end to the other, and I have this feeling, which never leaves me anymore, that I have been led.*[7]

Jayber had the sense of being led through confusing days in his career, the kind he could only fully understand later in life. He felt that his work as a barber—despite other plans he had as a youth—was a part of being drawn outward toward God in humility, and toward his neighbor in love.

Here Berry draws us toward the very center of a Christian understanding of calling: the love of God.

HIGHEST, COMMON, AND SPECIFIC CALLING

"Some people have a calling, Jeff. The rest of us just have jobs." My dad shared his blunt, yet honest, opinion over a phone call on my way home from work one day. I could hear the pain of doing work that he didn't particularly enjoy for most of his life. Calling felt to him like a conversation for the privileged or for ministers like his son.

As I remember our conversation, it was one I wish I could have back. I would have said, "Dad, calling is not about a perfect life. Calling means, first, to love God with all your heart, soul, mind, and strength, and to love your neighbor as yourself. This is the highest calling—one that you and I both share."

Historically, many Protestants have organized calling in terms of highest, common, and specific callings.[8] Our *highest calling* is first to be in direct relationship with God Himself.

Os Guinness puts it this way: "Calling is the truth that God calls us to himself so decisively that everything we are, everything we do, and everything we have is invested with a special devotion and dynamism lived out as a response to his summons and service."[9]

George Herbert, a seventeenth century English poet, expressed this same all-consuming vision of vocation in his poem *The Elixir*:

Teach me, my God and King,
In all things Thee to see,
And what I do in anything
To do it as for Thee.

Christians put the Great Commandment—to love God with all your heart, mind, soul, and strength, and to love your neighbor as yourself—at the center of conversations about calling. The first move in discerning our calling is not a skills inventory or job search, it is to move *outward* toward the majesty of God and a lifetime of service to Him (Col. 3:23).

COMMON:

Discerning your calling involves a skills inventory or job search.

vs.

UNCOMMON:

Discerning your calling is to move *outward* toward the majesty of God and a lifetime of service to Him.

Several years ago I invited a group of friends over to my friend Jack's house (isn't that what friends are for?) for an evening with pastor and author Skye Jethani. Skye shared his story of counseling people of all ages with questions about calling. He found something interesting. He said their prayers often sounded like, "God, this is what I want, so bless me." They tended to be inwardly focused: my work, my family, my opportunities. Yet he said his parishioners who adopted a not-my-will-but-Thy-will-be-done posture had a far easier time making choices about their next season of life. They were open-handed about several different visions of the future because in each scenario, Christ was still there.[10]

A *common calling* is to live the Christian life, a calling we hold "in common" with all believers. The apostle Paul urges the church at Ephesus to "live a life worthy of the calling you have received," and then paints a picture of the life of faith (Eph. 4–6).

English Puritans like Richard Baxter, a seventeenth-century pastor, took this common calling, summed up by the command to "love your neighbor as yourself," to mean choosing daily work that benefits the public good.

> The principal thing to be intended in the choice
> of a trade or calling for yourselves or children,
> is the service of God, and the public good, and
> therefore (other things being equal) that calling
> which [is most conducive] to the public good is to
> be preferred.[11]

Find a need, and meet it. It's not first (or even second) about your resume, your Meyers-Briggs profile, or even the hot job opportunities bubbling up on LinkedIn. Behind the love of God, think about the good of your community.

And be content not to be noticed but to simply live

out your life *coram Deo*, before the face of God. Albert Schweitzer, the French-German philosopher, physician, and humanitarian, once wrote, "There are no heroes of action: only heroes of renunciation."[12] This is the inverse logic of the gospel: the first will be last, and the last will be first. Empty yourself, and you will be filled. Die to yourself, and you will have life.

Finally, Scripture teaches the idea of a *specific calling*, which God gives to particular people at particular times. "For we are God's handiwork, created in Christ Jesus to do good works, which God prepared in advance for us to do" (Eph. 2:10). Some dub this "the call within the call," or the specific task people come to believe God has entrusted specifically to them.

Take for example Frances Perkins, the former Labor Secretary under Franklin Delano Roosevelt and key influencer behind the New Deal. Her commitment to God was forged early in her life at Mount Holyoke College, a school that sent hundreds of women to missionary service in places like India, Iran, and Africa. Yet it wasn't until 1911, when Perkins watched in horror as the Triangle Shirtwaist Factory burned to the ground, that her sense of calling was complete. As she witnessed hundreds of workers trapped by fire on the ninth floor and watched forty-seven people jump to their death to avoid being burned by the flames, she felt summoned by God to advocate for workers' rights for a lifetime.

Her specific calling led her into politics. She ultimately influenced FDR to commit to a broad array of social insurance policies: massive unemployment relief, minimum wage laws, the abolition of child labor, and, sure enough, a Social Security program for the elderly. (Here indeed is one of the beautiful parts of the original intention behind retirement—care for the elderly poor.)

Or take another example: George Washington Carver, one of the most significant scientists and inventors of American history. Carver was a botanist and agricultural innovator in the American South who called his lab at Tuskegee Institute "God's Little Workshop." Growing up enslaved in the South, Carver saw how Southern agriculture relied heavily on cotton, which both depleted the soil and was the backbone of the slave economy. Carver discovered that peanuts and soybeans could rejuvenate the soil. As he pursued his work as a botanist, he developed over 300 products from peanuts, 118 products from sweet potatoes, and over 500 dyes. His discoveries transformed the lives of poor Southern farmers, creating new markets and economic opportunities for African-Americans and whites alike. Here's how he described his calling:

> I know of no one who has ever worked with these roots in this way. I know of no book from which I can get this information, yet I will have no trouble in doing it. If this is not inspiration and information from a source greater than myself, or greater than any one has wrought up to the present time, kindly tell me what it is.[13]

For Carver, his life was animated by a lifelong love of God and science, the sweet voice of Christ, and the wonders of the natural world. On his grave it is written: "He could have added fortune to fame, but caring for neither, he found happiness and honor in being helpful to the world."

When our specific callings are put back into their proper place behind the love of God and neighbor, calling becomes less about finding a point on a map, and more about exploring the map for opportunities to serve others in freedom and love.

But questions still remain for those entering retirement and anxious to discern their own vocation: what should change from my career, and what should stay the same? What is unique about the senior years as opposed to young adulthood or mid-career? What is my calling for the next season of life?

RETIREMENT:
A SEASON OF WISDOM AND BLESSING

"This season of life is like fly fishing," said Fred Smith, the former president of The Gathering, an annual meeting of Christian philanthropists. "When I catch fish, I now don't need to keep them. I delight in releasing them. Catch and release—this is what retirement means for me."[14] Rather than holding on to past accomplishments and titles, Fred is simply content to *give* in his retirement. With his glasses, gentle demeanor, and trademark mustache, Fred is a man of uncommon *wisdom* and open-handed *blessing*.

Gordon Smith, the author of *Courage and Calling*, believes these two ideas—wisdom and blessing—are the biblical model for fruitful living in retirement. "To bless is simply to affirm the other, to take particular delight and joy in the other in a nonjudgmental or prescriptive manner," he writes.[15]

Smith tells the story of speaking at a family camp for Christian doctors and dentists. His own teenage sons loved the camp. Other men spent time with his sons teaching them to water ski or wind surf, as well as talking with them in quiet moments outdoors.

> These men seemed to have no other agenda than to enjoy the teens at the camp. And they had an immeasurable influence on my two sons. It seemed like they never used the word *should*, which all teens hate, and had no other plan than to bless my sons and the teens at the camp.[16]

The biblical patriarch Isaac blessed his son Jacob at the end of his life (Gen. 27:27–29), as did the elderly Jacob for his grandsons (Gen. 48:20). Not only was proximity to the young expected (something modern day 55+ retirement communities discourage), but the patriarchs had a critical influence on blessing the lives of coming generations.

Moreover, far from being an insult, the term "elder" was associated with wisdom, character, and leadership ability, the assumed fruit of experience and age. "Stand up in the presence of the aged" says Leviticus (19:32). The term "elder" (*zaqen*) is always used in the Old Testament as an indication of one's nobility. The elder taught wisdom at the city gate, the ancient place for public dialogue (Job 32:6–10).

In the New Testament, the term "elders" (*presbuteros*, stemming from *presbus*, elderly) was used in connection with the twelve apostles, the seventy disciples sent out by Jesus, and the earliest leaders of the church (1 Tim. 3:1–7, Titus 1:6–9). To be an elder was to hold a position of honor and public influence, particularly in the church.

Scripture is replete with elders playing a critical role in redemptive history. Sarah was 90 when she miraculously gave birth to Isaac; Moses was 80 and Aaron was 83 when they confronted Pharaoh; Anna, an 84-year-old widow who devoted herself to fasting, prayer, and worship, "gave thanks to God and spoke about the child [Jesus] to all who were looking forward to the redemption of Jerusalem" (Luke 2:38). Far from being whisked off to desert golf courses or Caribbean cruises, elders were sought out for time-tested wisdom (Prov. 16:31).

Yet Scripture also suggests a transfer of leadership to another generation, rather than clinging to past roles or titles. After retirement, Levitical priests were to pass on the heavy lifting of hauling the tabernacle (a tent) around the desert, and they were instead to "minister to their brothers in the tent of meeting by keeping guard," (Num. 8:26 ESV). Perhaps this is when they would "tell the next generation the praiseworthy deeds of the LORD, his power, and the wonders he has done" (Ps. 78:4).

This, however, does *not* assume older adults should "check out" or permanently hang up their cleats.

Countless people in their sixties, seventies, eighties, and even nineties have embraced opportunities to serve well for a lifetime. After Eugene Peterson retired as a pastor, he began publishing segments of *The Message*. The completed version of this bestselling version of the Bible was released in 2002 when Peterson was about 70. Toronto-based author Jane Jacobs kept publishing classic works on cities and urban life through her eighties. Senator Theodore Green didn't retire from the US Senate until he was 92. Sister Jean Dolores-Schmidt cheered from the stands when, as the chaplain of the University of Loyola-Chicago men's college basketball team, her 11th-seeded team made it to the Final Four in 2018. She was 98!

Yet the shape of fruitful service often changes later in life. Nelson Mandela became president of South Africa well after he was 65, but his role was more of grandfather to the new nation. His deputy ran nearly all the office of the president. He was an *elder* in the deepest sense of the word.

Ed Wekesser is 67 years old. He continues to coach Christian CEOs through a parachurch ministry called Convene. I asked him what has changed about his developing sense of vocation in his sixties. "Ah, that's simple," he said. "It's not about me anymore." He's now happy to simply forget himself and work for the success of others.

Retirement for people like Ed can be a season of "catch and release" that delights in open-handedly giving of the skills, talents, and experience accumulated over a lifetime to a world hungry for wisdom and blessing.

Six Questions to Discern Your Particular Calling

"Discerning our calling is like understanding our life as a string of pearls," says Brian Gray of Denver Institute for Faith & Work. "Each pearl on the string is one of our past jobs or life contexts. The string holding them together is that sense of calling that animates *how and why* we engaged each of those pearls." The best way to begin discerning God's specific call in your life is by looking at your past for patterns of how God has shaped you for His purposes.

During your sabbatical, gather with trusted friends or family to consider several important questions that can help you discern next steps for retirement.[17]

1. What is God doing in the world today that captures your imagination?

When you think of God, the Creator of all things who is reconciling the world to Himself in Christ, what captures your heart? Mentoring teenagers? Reading to grandkids? Leading a company? Writing novels? Volunteering with patients? What do you see in the world today that is good and should be encouraged, that's broken and in need of fixing, or missing and awaiting creation?

If the first step in discerning your calling is a step *outward* in love toward God and neighbor, where do you feel "grabbed by the collar" when you look out at the world today?

2. Who are you?

Self-knowledge is key to understanding your calling. Author Amy Sherman has put together an exercise called a "vocational power assessment."[18] The idea is that each of us has much more "power" than we often see. She asks:

- What unique positions at work have you held?
- What unique knowledge and expertise do you have?
- What platforms have you been given where people listen to you?
- What networks do you have?
- What skills do you have?
- What reputation or fame do you have that could be leveraged for others?

Self-knowledge is liberating. In it, we can acknowledge our limitations—and accept responsibility for the gifts and abilities that have been entrusted to us for the sake of the world God so loves (John 3:16).

3. What stage of life are you in?

In young adulthood, we learn to take responsibility for our lives. In midlife, the challenge is to accept ourselves for who we are, for better or worse. Older adulthood (retirement) is a season of letting go in order to bless and offer wisdom to a coming generation.

The questions here are: What do I need to let go of? And what (or *who*) do I need to cling to? What are the family obligations I have? Can I accept this season of life, and prepare for a different kind of fruitful contribution as I age?

4. What are your circumstances?

Name reality in a hope-filled way. Not nostalgically or regretfully, not bitterly or in thrall to the illusion of retirement bliss. But make it a practice to look at reality—your income, your relationships, your interests and talents, your limitations and opportunities—as the *only context in which you can fulfill your calling.*

COMMON:

Looking at reality nostalgically, regretfully, bitterly, or in thrall to the illusion of retirement bliss.

vs.

UNCOMMON:

Looking at reality as the only context in which you can fulfill your calling.

Jesus was God incarnate. Christianity teaches that the all-powerful Creator became a human being, replete with hunger and tears, imperfect parents and dull friends. It also meant that He could perfectly fulfill His calling and *not* do everything. There were people He healed—and thousands He didn't.

What are your family, work, financial, geographic, and other circumstances that will shape this season of life? And where might you have to say "no"?

5. What's the cross you've been called to bear?

Looking back on your life, what have been the moments of deep pain that have formed you?

As a senior in high school, I remember leaving an athletic club one Friday night. While my peers were spending time with their friends on a weekend, I remember walking to my car and looking up to outer space, feeling like darkness and loneliness were overtaking my soul. The pain was so acute I burst into tears, asking, "God, why should I be completely alone in the world? Is my life completely meaningless?"

Sobbing, I sat down on a curb. As I looked at the stars, I felt God almost audibly say, "I have called you by name. You are Mine."

I looked at the stars again, and now I saw their light. *There was light in the world*, I thought. *Now I know His name.*

I've always been haunted by a despair, a darkness that seems like all of my life and work will be useless and forgotten. It is a thorn in my flesh, a limp in my step. It's where I feel a deep brokenness and yet a deep burden. Today, giving people a renewed sense of purpose has become central to my calling and life work—and it was born out of my deepest pain.

How has suffering formed you? And what does it mean for how you will invest your retirement?

6. *What are you afraid of?*

Lisa is now in her second decade of retirement. A retired elementary school teacher, she's a lifelong learner. Once a week she cares for her three grand-daughters, bringing science experiments, educational activities, and an almost super-human patience to her son's home.

On a recent trip to visit a fellow retiree, she saw that her friend's life was almost completely busied with forms of entertainment: classes, movies, vacations, and strenuous exercise.

"Why do you suppose she hikes so much?" I asked. As we chatted, Lisa said, "Jeff, she's eight years older than her husband. Now in her late 70s, she's always felt guilty about this. I think she's afraid of dying and leaving her husband alone. So she does anything to stay fit and not think about what's coming."

What are you afraid of in this season of life? Death? Loneliness? Irrelevance? Poor health? Poverty? Adult children who aren't flourishing?

In order to live fully in retirement, we must name our fears, and offer them to Christ in prayer. Allow God to say, "Don't be afraid, for I am with you. I will surely be with you to the very end of the age" (see Isa. 41:10; Matt. 28:16–20).

Writing Your Eulogy—and Your Future

Writing your will can be a morbid experience. Who really wants to think about who will get my stuff once I'm in a coffin? Writing your eulogy, however, has the power to shape the next thirty years of your life.

A eulogy is a speech in praise of someone, usually someone who has just died. Have you ever thought about what others will say about you at your funeral?

"What mark will I have left on those in my life after I'm gone?" I've thought about this probably more than is healthy for a man barely at the "midlife" mark (it's a part of that darkness streak I mentioned). My great fear is that people will say, "He was successful, and did many successful things," but in their hearts they'll think, *but he did not love us.*

I see the faces of my four daughters flash before my eyes when I lose my temper. I see the face of my wife, as she waits at the kitchen table for me to ask about her day, but I'm too tired to pay attention to her. I see the faces of my co-workers who congratulate me for being "successful," yet I remember my relative relational cluelessness as harsh and stinging—perhaps even demanding.

When I think about that day, I ask God to fill in all my weaknesses and shortcomings. The central prayer of my life has become: *Christ, make me more like Yourself.*

As an activity to help me clarify my own sense of calling right now, I recently wrote my own eulogy, a statement of what I left behind—and what I will commit myself to today. As you think about the roles of your life—mother, child, worker, citizen, member of a church—I'd recommend the activity for you as you consider your calling for the next season of life.

Here's mine:

As an entrepreneur, Jeff left behind a network of institutions and people committed to healing Christ's broken world.

As a writer, Jeff left behind a written testimony to Christ's great love for the world.

As a husband and father, Jeff left behind a family committed to loving the Lord their God with all of their hearts, minds, souls, and strength, and to loving their neighbors as themselves.

The question, then, for all of us is: *What does that mean for my work?*

Chapter 4

Work

*Each of you should use whatever gift you have
received to serve others, as faithful stewards
of God's grace in its various forms.*

1 Peter 4:10

For many, the thought of working in retirement surfaces feelings of both pain and possibility.

On one side is weariness. In *Habits of the Heart*, sociologist Robert Bellah interviewed executives, government employees, school teachers, and small-business people on how they felt about retirement. He found they were "sick of working," hated "the pressure," had "paid their dues," and "wanted to get out of the rat race." So they chose to retire to "lifestyle enclaves," as Bellah puts it, or retirement communities built around leisure and consumption, usually unrelated to the world of work.[1]

Today Gallup reports that 87 percent of the world's workforce is disengaged from their work. If retirement offers a way out of painful or unsatisfying jobs, it's no wonder most choose to retire as soon as they can.[2]

On the other side, however, is a spark of energy, enthusiasm, and genuine curiosity about new possibilities for work in retirement.

My friend Dr. Mark Roberts leads the Max De Pree Center for Leadership at Fuller Theological Seminary. In a series of focus groups he conducted with recent retirees, he paraphrased many who said, "I felt like it was time to let younger people lead; but I still have gas left in the tank. I'm not ready to be completely done yet." For many, retirement offers a budding hope for work that better aligns with calling, yet is less subject to the deadline-driven pressure of their careers.

Caught between "by the sweat of your brow" and the creative "work of your hands," millions of baby boomers are dipping their feet in the waters of working in retirement.

After a "purposeful pause," Barry Rowan decided to go back into business working as the CFO of two public companies. "I came to see that the purpose of business is to bring about a better society as seen through the eyes of God," Rowan said. After his sabbatical, his work was endowed with renewed peace and purpose. He saw his work as not just a way to make money, but a God-given opportunity to build businesses around "responsible value creation, creating an environment where employees can flourish, serving customers, and being good corporate citizens." Now in his sixties, he is also seeking to mentor young,

Christian business leaders. "I don't think I'll ever fully retire," says Rowan.[3]

A 2016 report from the Bureau of Labor Statistics shows that the proportion of Americans over age 65 who were employed, either full time or part time climbed from 12.8 percent in 2000 to 18.8 percent in 2016.[4] Some call it "unretirement"—others, a "purposeful retirement."

Today a growing number of boomers are making a shift from a *Let's vacation* mentality to a life of service; from purposelessness to reengagement; from consumption to "wisdom and blessing;" from free-floating days to committed work for the well-being of their neighbors over a lifetime.

The possibilities are exciting—but the challenges are real as well. In a 2016 report by the Federal Reserve, 38 percent of adults aged 60 or over said they planned to continue working in retirement. Yet a Gallup poll found that only 4 percent of retirees worked until age 70 or beyond, and only 7 percent had income from a job.[5] Why the disparity?

Research shows that health problems, age discrimination, caring for loved ones, social class, and the lack of quality work arrangements for older adults today all help explain why far fewer baby boomers actually make it to finding and enjoying a new line of work in retirement.

As you start making your plan for working in retirement, new questions need to be answered: What is God's original design for work? Why do people choose to work in retirement? What are the challenges older adults face while working later in life, and how can they be overcome? What questions should I ask when making my own plan for working after retirement?

MADE IN THE IMAGE OF A MAKER

Christian faith offers a corrective to contemporary views of work in retirement. On one side of the cultural spectrum, *work in retirement is seen as a curse.*

This story about work is prevalent today in the financial industry. In 2018, E-Trade, a financial services company, ran a 2018 Super Bowl commercial featuring people working into their eighties. "Dropping sick beats, they call me DJ Nana," says an 85-year-old granny at a turntable in a dance club. The refrain is sung to Day-O (the Banana Boat song): "I'm 85 and I want to go home." An elderly man picks up a fire hose—and is propelled across the room. A small, white-haired woman is dropping UPS packages, clumsily. The punch line: "Over 1/3 of Americans have no retirement savings. This is getting old." The tag line: "Don't get mad. Get E-Trade."

This commercial points to a disturbing economic reality for America, as well as the stewing resentment of the *I can't afford the vacation* camp. But it also suggests that if you work in retirement, you've failed. It's as if the financial prophets of Wall Street are saying, "Who sinned, that you are working so late in life? You or your financial advisor?"

For many, the story is that work is just something

you do until you make enough money. Canadian-born blogger Peter Adeney, known as "Mr. Money Mustache" and a leader of the FIRE (Financial Independence, Retire Early) movement, advocates austere living in order to, as quickly as possible, stop working and live off of investment income. Work is seen as an unholy trade of hours for dollars, and its central purpose is . . . to work no more.

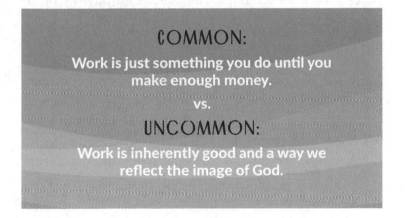

COMMON:

Work is just something you do until you make enough money.

vs.

UNCOMMON:

Work is inherently good and a way we reflect the image of God.

In stark contrast, ancient Christians and Hebrews believed *work is inherently good and a way we reflect the image of God.* In Genesis, God's creative activity is called *work.* "By the seventh day God had finished the work he had been doing," and then He pauses to evaluate what He's done and calls it *good* (2:2–3). When God creates humanity, He also gives them work to do as a way of reflecting His own character. Gardening (manual labor) and naming the animals (intellectual labor) were part of an original, unstained world (Gen. 2:15, 19).

Work "should be the full expression of the worker's faculties, the thing in which he finds spiritual, mental, and bodily satisfaction, and the medium in which he offers himself to God,"[6] writes Dorothy Sayers.

On the other side of the spectrum, our secular culture tends to *idolize work and success*. Pastor Timothy Keller writes, "Many modern people seek a kind of salvation— self-esteem and self-worth—from career success. This leads us to seek only high-paying, high-status jobs, and to 'worship' them in perverse ways."[7] The essence of work in a secular culture is about individual achievement and personal fulfillment. In this framework, work in retirement becomes another way to prove individual worth. Those caught in this web struggle in retirement with letting go and finding identity apart from formal job titles.

Again, in contrast to this view, for Christians, *work is an expression of love* because it's the principal way we serve the needs of our neighbors. Just after World War II, theologian Elton Trueblood said, "A Church which seeks to lift our sagging civilization will preach the *principle of vocation* in season and out of season. The message is that the world is one, secular and sacred, and that the chief way to serve the Lord is in our daily work."[8] Through our work, thought Trueblood, we provide legal systems, electricity, healthcare, clean water, groceries, and innumerable goods and services that provide for the needs of our neighbors. Work is the primary avenue for fulfilling Christ's command to love your neighbor as yourself.

COMMON:

Work in a secular culture is about individual achievement and personal fulfillment.

vs.

UNCOMMON:

Work is an expression of love because it's the principal way we serve the needs of our neighbors.

For Christians, work is fundamentally about contribution to others, not compensation; it's an expression of our identity, but not the source of our identity; it's about serving others, not personal success.

If work is an act of love, whether paid or unpaid, then for Christians, work is an activity that should continue, in different forms, as long as we're alive—even in retirement.

WORK AND RETIREMENT

Susan Cole is a 56-year-old music educator who taught elementary students for more than two decades before retiring. Suffering from fibromyalgia, the long, high-energy days had taken their toll on her health. "It was a hard decision for me," she said. "I felt like the job both tore me down and built me up." She decided to continue working part time as a piano teacher at a local music school. Just after Susan's retirement, her mother broke her femur and another family member needed her care. "My availability was totally a God thing," she recalls. "He was calling me to both care for my students and my family in this season. I was needed here. But I don't ever see myself giving up teaching." She saw God's hand in allowing her to continue to work part time while caring for her family.

Many must make a choice in retirement: Do I want to volunteer, work full time, work part time, or not work at all?

Gene Edward Veith, a prolific author on vocation, retired in 2018. "I expected certain people to give me a hard time," Veith said. "'So, the author of three books on vocation is retiring,' I could imagine them saying."[9] Yet after forty-nine years in the workforce, he realized that his vocation included work—but not only paid work. He had a calling to family (as father and son), the church (as a Christian), and the state (as a citizen). He still writes and teaches but has made space for other commitments in addition to his work as a professor emeritus.

The Christian concept of vocation offers great freedom in expressing the love of God and neighbor through work over a lifetime. Lynn Haanen (my mother) expresses her vocation of teaching by caring for her eight grandkids on a regular basis (to the deep gratitude of her son). Sue Ellen King (from chapter 2) decided to go back to work part time as a nurse when her replacement went on maternity leave. One couple I know decided to taper their work schedule as they aged. At 65 they worked four days a week; at 70 they went to three days a week; and at 75 they went to two days a week. They stopped working at ages 77 and 78.

Though the Bible suggests deep liberty in choosing different kinds of work as men and women become "elders," what decisions in retirement would be explicitly "out" for a Christian? I see two clear prohibitions regarding work later in life:

Idleness

"Slothfulness casts into a deep sleep, and an idle person will suffer hunger" (Prov. 19:15 ESV). Though often not mentioned from today's pulpits, sloth is one of the "seven deadly sins." The older writers saw inaction or laziness as a deeper sign of spiritual apathy. The Bible says, "The one who is unwilling to work shall not eat" (2 Thess. 3:10–11). This may sound harsh to those entering into retirement. But the logic is that everybody would "work quietly and . . . earn their own living" so that they "may have something to share with anyone in need" (2 Thess. 3:12; Eph. 4:28 ESV). We must honestly ask: When does rest or recreation morph into idleness inside the contemporary experience of retirement?

Self-Focused Pleasure

To those who live only for eating, drinking, and entertainment, the apostle Paul reminds them that their bodies were purchased at the price of Christ's blood (1 Cor. 6:19–20). Enjoyment of the created world is good (1 Tim. 6:17). But a life that revolves around the pleasures of the flesh is evil (Rom. 8:6). Again, we must ask, when does taking a rest from work turn into a life revolving around entertainment and pleasure?

The Bible calls Christians to never tire of doing good (Gal. 6:9), because "the Son of Man came not to be served but to serve, and to give his life as a ransom for many" (Mark 10:45). Though work changes over a lifetime, as we've discussed, there's nothing to suggest that work should completely cease at 62, 65, or 70. In fact, many entering into retirement decide to continue the "pearl of their calling" into the sunset of their lives.

"Yes, I'm 91," said Ellen Snyder, a lifelong hospital volunteer living in Greenwood Village, Colorado, "but why should I stop doing what I'm called to, just because I'm a certain age?"

Ever since World War II, Ellen Snyder volunteered in hospitals as her daily work. She first wrapped bandages for soldiers and then volunteered at Craig Hospital in Englewood, Colorado. When she turned sixty, her husband retired, and they moved to Arizona. But Ellen felt uncomfortable. She took golf lessons, had long lunches with her friends, yet she still felt like something was missing. "I was bored," she said flatly.

When she returned to Colorado from Arizona, she kept feeling led to volunteer at the St. Francis Center, a day center for the homeless in Denver. She had doubts. "How can I drive way downtown by myself?" she thought. "No, I don't want to do it, I said to myself. But I kept feeling this nudging." One day, she listened to the nudging and drove to the St. Francis Center. "I just felt this is where I'm supposed to be," she said when she arrived.

For Ellen, the reason she decided to continue her life work, albeit in a different context, was simple: "I enjoy serving because it took me outside of myself. I was equipped by the Lord to help somebody else. I think love is the bottom line—love your neighbor as yourself. It's easy to love."[10]

For Ellen, her commitment to working on behalf of her neighbors was an overflow of divine love.

OVERCOMING CHALLENGES

Working in retirement, however, is filled with possible challenges that you should anticipate as you start planning your next season of life:

You'll have to make a countercultural decision to work in retirement.

If 19 percent of people over age 65 were working at least part time in 2017, that means 81 percent weren't. Bucking the trend of increased golfing or television watching is not easy (the average retiree spends four hours per day watching television!).[11] If your friends travel three months a year, and you limit your travel to three weeks a year, it will feel strange. It might also feel strange filling out job applications to work for people half your age.

But working in retirement is a countercultural trend

that is becoming more common as more baby boomers are seeking professional community and a deeper sense of purpose in retirement. As Eleanor Roosevelt once said, "It is not more vacation that we need—it is more vocation."

Society doesn't often provide flexible arrangements to work in retirement.

Sociologists like Matilda White Riley have developed the idea of "structural lag."[12] She says that social institutions—like corporations or policies—are resistant to change and lag behind cultural trends. One example is that when older adults look for meaningful work, they often find systems built for a complete cessation of work at retirement—or part-time jobs that are entry level and don't leverage valuable skills. One survey from the Transamerica Center for Retirement Studies (TCRS) found that 47 percent of workers envision a phased transition into retirement, but only 5 percent of employers offer a formal phased retirement program.[13]

What can be done? Many older adults go to a different employer, freelance, or start their own business. Some who are self-employed can phase into part-time work. But for most, the fit between talent, time commitment, and lower-than-expected pay is awkward in a society built around a previous generation's gold-watch-and-pension model of retirement.

Health and family issues
impact work more frequently in retirement.

Many find that staying healthy is one of the most important factors in being able to work in retirement. Nearly 40 percent of workers retire for unexpected health reasons.[14] Staying healthy is critical to being able to work and serve well for a lifetime.

Ageism is a reality.

"I quickly found that with being older, people don't call me for an interview," said Sarajul Islam, a 60-year-old man living in the UK. "When contacted personally or over the phone, a few recruiters have directly said, 'We don't call back old people.'"[15]

Often older adults are passed up for jobs or opportunities because of false assumptions about age. Though outlawed in most countries, tacit ageism is still active in many companies and cultures and must be challenged by learning new skills, exceeding employer expectations, and overcoming stereotypes.

Social class and income
will deeply impact your view of work in retirement.

There are two very different visions for work, depending on which of the two very different Americas you inhabit.[16] If you have a college degree and worked in the professions, you're far more likely to work in retirement—even though you may not have to financially. The challenge in retirement will be resisting the temptation to splurge on grandkids, travel too much, or otherwise live for yourself. If you enjoyed your career, you likely wouldn't mind doing it part time well into retirement.[17]

But if you're a part of America's working class, working in retirement may feel very different. Doug Muder grew up in farm country, Illinois. As a kid he remembered his dad working in a factory that made cattle feed. He "came home stinking of fish oil," Muder recalls. It was a good job in that it paid the bills, but his dad had a very different relationship to his work than Muder did as a journalist. Muder offers an important insight on work in retirement:

> Here's what sums it up to me: When professionals retire, we keep dabbling. The retired newspaper editor in my hometown still writes. When the professor retires, he'll keep reading journals and going to talks. But in the thirty years since my Dad took early retirement, he has never brought home some fish oil and mixed up a batch of cattle feed in the garage. When you retire from Wal-Mart, you don't set up a bar-code scanner in the basement, just to stay busy. You do that stuff for money, and when they stop paying you, you never, ever do it again.[18]

Working-class Americans experience more barriers than their college-educated peers when attempting to reengage work in retirement. For example,

1. Physical labor is much harder to do at 65 or 70, making reentering the workforce especially

difficult for those in the trades or manual labor.
2. Wages are likely to be lower for working-class Americans, providing less incentive to work.
3. If you didn't enjoy your work or you'd need significant education to find a new job after retirement, the road back to work will be blocked with more obstacles.

I'm *not* saying that working as a carpenter or electrician is intrinsically harder or less satisfying than working as a banker. (I think many who spend their lives in front of screens would agree the opposite is true!) But for many lower-wage jobs, often worked without much choice in the first place, it's often difficult to muster the enthusiasm to jump back into work after retirement.

MAKING A WRITTEN PLAN

Considering these challenges, writing down your plan for work after retirement can be the key to making dreams a reality.

Rebecca Sahr, a 61-year-old owner of her own accounting business in Colorado, thinks the biggest problem with achieving a fulfilling retirement is a lack of planning. "I've seen so many friends," she says, "completely fail at retirement because they weren't intentional. They didn't write anything down, didn't talk with friends—they planned to save for retirement, but not what to do once they did retire."

"Planning is an unnatural process; it's much more fun to do something," wrote twentieth-century businessman Sir John Harvey-Jones. "And the nicest thing about not planning is that failure comes as a complete surprise rather than being preceded by a period of worry and depression."[19]

Unfortunately, far too many people are completely surprised—and underwhelmed—by retirement because they didn't accept 91-year-old Ellen Snyder's advice: "Be sure before you decide to retire you know what you might do in the future so you're not just sitting there thinking, 'What do I want to do?'"

As you make a written plan to work after retirement (feel free to write in the margins of this book!), you'll eventually have to answer five questions:

1. What is God calling me to?

In Keith and Kristin Getty's modern hymn *In Christ Alone*,[20] they sing about God's love and peace and the end of our fear and striving. As you enter the elder phase of your life, and your youthful strivings for achievement, position, and power are quieted by the knowledge that Christ has already finished the ultimate work of redemption, where do you sense God's leading to serve?

As you plan work in retirement, you'll need to make hard choices. You cannot do everything. But neither is God calling you to do nothing. Dying to the possibilities of what will never be also gives you the freedom to pursue what God is giving uniquely to you.

2. What will be different from my career? What will be similar?

Gary VanderArk, the not-so-retired neurosurgeon I mentioned in the first chapter, continued to do his work as a doctor throughout his life. Because he always felt a sense of continuity between his calling and his work, he decided to continue his full-time job as a doctor well into his seventies.

Others, however, decide that retirement is a time to pick up the pearl of vocation that they've sensed during their career, but have never fully explored. Keith Gordon, a 61-year-old retired engineer, decided to use his skills to become a high school math teacher through a program called Transition to Teaching, "which helps longtime workers nearing retirement move into second careers teaching math or science."[21]

Working in retirement can be a chance to continue parts of your career or to make a change completely. Which will you choose? And, more importantly, *why?* What's driving you?

3. How many hours per week will I work?

"I liked your speech, but you missed something," a kind gentleman in his late sixties said to me after a talk I gave in Virginia. "I just don't have the same energy level I used to. I still have several accounting clients, but now I take naps every afternoon."

Working after retirement should take into consideration the realities of aging, even while embracing what you *can* do. But don't let this frustrate you.

Though energy levels will obviously vary from person to person, fruitful contribution as an elder, mentor, and influencer can bear deep, lasting fruit.

Retirement can be an opportunity to bring greater sanity to rhythms of work and rest, even while continuing to contribute fruitfully to your community for decades to come. You'll need to decide, how many hours per day or week do I want to work in retirement?

4. What kinds of work do I want to experiment with?

If you're planning on making a career change, prepare yourself. Ask a veteran in the field or company you're interested in before making a final choice. Richard Baxter, the seventeenth-century Puritan pastor, wrote to those contemplating job choices, "Choose no calling (especially if it be of public consequence) without the advice of some judicious, faithful persons of that calling."[22] Barry Rowan asked many of his friends before hopping into a new job. Consider asking your community about new opportunities during sabbatical.

In addition, consider your opportunity, abilities, and affinities before choosing a new job. What opportunities are right in front of you? What are your abilities—ones that friends, family and coworkers have seen in you? And what do you *want* to do?

Finally, be courageous. Be willing to experiment with new lines of work, new jobs, or new fields of endeavor.

5. *How will I balance and embrace my different callings in retirement?*

I don't believe work is the only calling we have. We're called to be children, parents, and spouses; we're called to be citizens of our communities; we're called to be members of the church.

As you consider how to spend your time in retirement, and what role paid work will play in your next season of life, how is God calling you to love each of your various "neighbors" as yourself? Caring for an ailing parent full time—and not working—may be exactly what God is calling you to do right now. Your work is not the fullness of your vocation. As Mother Teresa once said, "Many people mistake our work for our vocation. Our [primary] vocation is the love of Jesus."[23]

Readiness to respond to God's voice is the heartbeat of making choices about work over a lifetime.

WORK AND HOPE

On March 24, 1980, Oscar Romero, the archbishop of San Salvador, El Salvador, was martyred while celebrating Mass in a small chapel of the cancer hospital where he lived. As a tireless champion of the poor, Romero risked more for his calling later in life.

A piece sometimes called the Oscar Romero Prayer, and often attributed to him, is actually an excerpt from a homily written by Fr. Ken Untener. In "A Future Not Our Own," Untener reminds us of the deep, lasting hope for our work. He acknowledges that, in our brief lifetime, we accomplish just a "fraction of the magnificent enterprise that is God's work." While we are unable to complete every goal, objective, and mission, we do plant seeds. And this is why it's important to take the long view: the work we aren't able to finish is an opportunity for "God's grace to enter and do the rest."[24]

The fact that we may not live to see the fruit of our efforts underscores the difference between human beings and the Creator: "We are workers, not master builders; ministers, not messiahs. . . . We are prophets of a future not our own."[25]

This is the posture of working in retirement that the Christian church can offer the world. We take the long view. We plant seeds, knowing others will harvest. We set foundations for others to build on. We recognize we are "workers, not master builders; ministers, not messiahs. We are prophets of a future not our own." We are not world changers. God is the only and lasting world changer. We are simply servants, whose hearts are transfixed by a deeper hope.

Christian people can commit to *working on behalf of their neighbors over a lifetime* because they can see a world where God has finally wiped away every tear from their eyes. They embrace what the Talmud says: "[It's] not thine to complete the work, yet neither art thou free to lay it down."[26] If you're alive, God has a purpose for you, yet it's one that will only be fully accomplished when His kingdom comes.

COMMON:
We are world changers.
vs.
UNCOMMON:
We are simply servants.

Because of such hope, we can look at the next twenty or thirty years in retirement, and humbly embrace the apostle's words, "Each of you should use whatever gift you have received to serve others, as faithful stewards of God's grace in its various forms" (1 Peter 4:10).

Part II:

WISDOM

Chapter 5

Time

Teach us to number our days,
that we may gain a heart of wisdom.

Psalm 90:12

"The first thing you have to know about retirement," says Allan Spies, a 68-year-old retired US West executive, "is that you could live another forty years."

Spies recalled a conversation he had with his pastor when he was on the cusp of an early retirement in his fifties. The pastor reminded Spies of all the time he had ahead of him. As Spies started to spend his newfound time, he was also jarred by how much his schedule changed. "The other thing you've got to know," he says, "is that suddenly your clock changes."

Many enter retirement busied and harried from the last few months of work. Then, like jumping off a moving train, the forward momentum comes to an abrupt halt. Weekdays melt into weekends. Long breakfasts can become early lunches. The time that was lacking in the pressure of raising a family and pursuing a career now floods into a quiet home.

After an initial honeymoon period, many early retirees find themselves quickly looking for structure to their days and weeks. "I had to do something," says Lynn Haanen about her early retirement. "My days lacked a schedule and a sense of purpose." Initially relieved to leave the "grind" of teaching third graders, Lynn gloried in finally having time to herself. But eventually, she realized her weeks were amorphous and needing structure.

Her life in retirement had traded the stopwatch for the lava lamp, with hours and days slowly blobbing into each other without direction.

For millions of Americans, early retirement can feel like entering Dr. Seuss's "The Waiting Place." In his classic *Oh, the Places You'll Go!*, Seuss warns about "a most useless place" for "people just waiting."[1]

Fear of being caught in a useless cycle of waiting leads many to backfill their days with activities, errands, and "busy work" to avoid the anxiety of purposelessness. Time becomes a burden, something to be used up, like too much corn overflowing a silo after harvest. "Oh, I stay busy," becomes the anxious response to "How's retirement?"

New research shows that human longevity is giving people a newfound abundance of years—a change few have planned for.

TIME, TIME, AND MORE TIME

In 1900, the average male could expect to live to age 46 and the average female, age 48. Today, "if you are now 20 you have a 50 per cent chance of living to more than 100; if you are 40 you have an even chance of reaching 95; if you are 60, then a 50 per cent chance of making 90 or more."[2] Over the last two hundred years, life expectancy has increased at a rate of more than two years every decade.

If you retire at age 65, this means that you will have an even chance of living twenty-five years beyond retirement. (Studies show that half of Americans retire from ages 61–65, and a full two-thirds of Americans are out of the full-time workforce by age 66.[3]) If you exercise, eat healthy, minimize alcohol consumption, and have generally healthy relationships, plan on at least three more decades of life.

In Lynda Gratton and Andrew Scott's fascinating book *The 100 Year-Life*, they see drastic changes coming to the world in the next fifty years as the population ages—and lives longer than ever before.

Out of necessity, people will work into their seventies and eighties. Gratton and Scott ask their MBA students at the London Business School, "If you live 100 years, save around 10 per cent of your income and want to retire on 50 per cent of your final salary, at what age will you be able to retire?" The answer: in your eighties. Human longevity is changing the equation of financial planners and government pensions.[4]

There will be new jobs, skills, and a new need for life-long education. If you live to 100 and work into your seventies and eighties, the economy will likely have been completely transformed since your high school, undergraduate, or graduate education. The need to learn new job skills—and to take time to reinvest in your education—will rise in importance.[5]

Family and home relationships will be transformed. Four generations living at the same time will become a norm and, as baby boomer budgets are stressed, intergenerational living will become commonplace.[6]

People will be younger for longer. With advances in medical technology, many reporters and social observers have said "60 is the new 50." Though we should carry a healthy skepticism of the "forever young" narrative of our culture (as we'll explore in the next chapter), we also shouldn't ignore the fact that people are now living longer, healthier lives than ever before.[7]

One of the most fascinating changes already happening due to human longevity is that the three-stage life is starting to lose its meaning. For generations, it was assumed that you lived in three stages: first education, then employment, and finally retirement. (Many Christian books have adopted this paradigm and called retirement a "third third," or a "third calling." Other books have assumed that "aging" and "retirement" are the same topic, which is no longer true. "Old age" is something that—for most—will happen decades later.) But today, the seasons of life dedicated to work, family, education, and rest will become more fluid. You might start a new career at 50, become an undergraduate at 60, and a great-grandparent at 70.

Christianity can, and should, dump a bucket of cold water on much of a secular culture's near-worship of the medical technology that has elongated our lives. "From dust we came," we say on Ash Wednesday, "and to dust we shall return."

But Christian thinkers, pastors, and leaders also need to lead the way in communicating that retirement is quite simply no longer a life stage "preparing for the end," but instead a contemporary social construct that allows men and women to prepare for a new season of life.

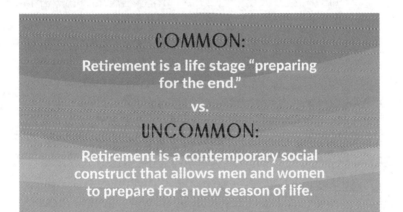

COMMON:
Retirement is a life stage "preparing for the end."

vs.

UNCOMMON:
Retirement is a contemporary social construct that allows men and women to prepare for a new season of life.

We'll have to start asking better questions: What will you do with all this time in retirement? What might Christian faith say about these newfound hours, days, weeks, months, and years that lie ahead?

WHEELS, WALLS, AND STORIES—CHOOSING
YOUR VIEW OF TIME

Eastern religions, such as Hinduism and Buddhism (and many New Age philosophies) view time as circular. For example, in Hinduism the wheel of *samsara,* or reincarnation, is a continuous cycle in which at death the soul is carried into a new body, whether human or animal, based on their behavior (or *karma*) in this life. In this view, time is most like a wheel that keeps revolving, without beginning or end. There is no urgency, because time is infinite.

In secular humanism, time is more like a wall. A materialist view of time sees the sun eventually expanding, burning up the earth, and human beings simply being no more. This view of time is *annihilationist.* Therefore, views of time in this worldview tend toward making "YOLO" (you only live once) decisions. This could be either "make a big impact while you can" or "let's eat and drink, for tomorrow we die." Either way, if we're just cosmic accidents, enjoy consciousness while you can.

Christianity has a unique view of time. Time is linear. History has a beginning (Gen. 1) and end (Matt. 28:20). Time for Christians is like a story, with God as the Author. God is moving human history to its glorious culmination in the judgment of man, the resurrection of the dead, and the renewed heavens and earth. And once human history ends, a new story begins for immortal men and women living and reigning with Christ in the heavenly city. Today we are living in the *middle* of the story. Because of this, each moment is endowed with a *gravitas* because our actions today will have a ripple effect forever.

In one sense, time for Christians is brief, and each moment is vital. Because we are but a vapor in the scope of history (James 4:14, Ps. 90:10), we are to make the most of every opportunity (Eph. 5:16). But in another sense, time is eternal. "When we've been there ten thousand years, bright shining as the sun," says the famous hymn "Amazing Grace." "We've no less days, to sing God's praise, than when we'd first begun." There is no concern for our mortal bodies or limited time on earth, but rather a deep peace that God is the One who will ultimately bring the story to its dramatic climax.

When we look at spending time in retirement, whether that be four years or forty, Christianity weds urgency with peace. Ultimately, time for Christians is a *gift* to be cherished.

Planning Your Time in Retirement

What would your 90-year-old self say to the decisions you are making today?

It's a vulnerable, thought-provoking question. Could your present-day decisions stand up to the scrutiny of your future self? Or to put it another way, if you were viewing your current calendar—days, weeks, and months—from the perspective of those giving your funeral eulogy, would you keep doing those activities?

What would change?

There are two categories of time spent that balloon

in retirement: home improvement (two hours and thirty-two minutes daily) and watching TV. The average retiree spends *four hours per day* watching TV, or twenty-eight hours a week . . . 1,460 hours per year.[8] (One study found that watching TV or videos for an average of six hours per day can shorten a viewer's life by up to five years.[9]) In other words, most retirees trade work for sitting in front of a TV.

Can we do better?

Time in retirement is a precious gift, and several practices will help you best steward that gift.

Days & Weeks

Decide what's important.

Before you break out the calendar, decide what's genuinely important to you. Review your responses to the previous chapters' questions on calling and work and begin with a list of things you want to accomplish this week or month. "Not every need is a calling," my former New Testament professor Bill Klein used to say.

But what *are* your genuine callings—and when do you want to see them accomplished? Peter Drucker, the father of modern management, said it best: "Efficiency is doing the thing right. Effectiveness is doing the right thing." Deciding on what's important, and making a plan to do it, is the path toward effectiveness and impact.

Make a plan.

This may seem like an obvious place to start. But for most, it's revolutionary. Before you start your day or week, write down: what needs to get done today? What are the top three things I have to get done this week? Then move your big goals to daily and weekly appointments. If they appear on your calendar, it's far more likely they'll get done.

Front-load your days with "maker" tasks over "manager" tasks.

Tech investor Paul Graham makes the helpful distinction between two kinds of schedules: "maker schedule" and "manager schedule."[10] Maker tasks are essentially creative. They are right brain activities that require abstract thought, concentration, and large blocks of time.

Manager tasks are "get-'er-done" types of items: sending an email, hanging a picture, visiting the hospital, teaching a lesson. These are left brain activities that require a tight schedule and a clear task list.

When I plan my schedule, I try to prioritize "maker" tasks in the first third of the day, knowing that the afternoon—when my circadian rhythms naturally want to make me fall asleep—are a better time for less challenging activities. (Like taking a nap!)

If you make this a habit, you'll find yourself making progress on the big goals you've set for yourself, like writing a memoir or becoming an architect, and not only the smaller errands that tend to fill our days.

Set deadlines and embrace accountability.

This may sound like something your former boss might say. But setting real deadlines, and telling people about them, is the only way to actually accomplish goals *you have deemed important.* Goals without deadlines are simply wishful thinking.

Make a not-to-do list.

Jim Collins, international business guru and author of the bestselling *Good to Great,* gives the sagacious advice: make a "Stop Doing" list. He says to decide what's unimportant on your task list, and then simply don't do it. Watch and see if anybody misses that task not getting done.

Shut off the TV . . . and the internet.

This is perhaps the most important part of planning your weekly time. Social media, the latest movie, or the most recent news article will likely add nothing to your soul, your work, or your family.

Steven Sample, former president of the University of Southern California and the author of *The Contrarian's Guide to Leadership,* read through many of the world's great classics during his busy tenure as a university president simply by shutting off the news and committing to reading a classic book for just a half hour per day.

We live in an age of distraction. But we also know that most of us need the internet to communicate with family or friends—or we will simply want to watch the occasional movie on a screen. In order to not let media distract you from your calling, consider planning out screen time. For example, set email time from 4–4:30 p.m., or weekly movie time on Fridays from 7–8:30 p.m.

Small decisions that push away the noise go a long way toward "redeeming the time" (Eph. 5:16 KJV).

Months & Years

Plan in seasons for new, long-term commitments.

If you are going to live another twenty, thirty, or forty years, this means you can also plan in new seasons and long-term commitments. Once or twice a year, you may consider taking a silent retreat to consider learning a new skill, pursuing a new career, or moving next to kids in order to help care for grandkids for a season.

Ancient Greeks had two words for time: *chronos* and *kairos*. While *chronos* is chronological time, marked by seconds, minutes, or hours, *kairos* means the right, critical, or opportune moment. Christ recognized the difference between "harvest time" or God-led "seasons" and the mere passing of hours (John 7:6).

In retirement, as you listen to God's voice, when is the right time to undertake a new adventure? And when is the right time to sit with a friend who has cancer? When is God calling you to mentor, and when is God calling you to start a new course of learning?

Cross-reference your past schedule with your statement about calling.

As you take a look at the past months and even year,

cross-reference your activities with your written statements about calling. Do they align? If not, why? What needs to change moving forward?

Plan in a season for another sabbatical.

As you reengage the world of work, you eventually may consider planning another sabbatical. God told the Israelites to let the land lie fallow one year out of every seven years (Lev. 25). Not only do our weeks need rhythms of work and rest, but so do our years. Such a 6-to-1 rhythm of work and rest may have been God's intent for our careers from the beginning.

THE GIFT OF TIME

In Charles Dickens's classic *A Christmas Carol*, Ebenezer Scrooge is led by the black-clad Ghost of Christmas Yet To Come to his very own grave.

The ghost silently points to him, to the grave, and back to him again. Old Scrooge begs, "Spirit! Hear me! I am not the man I was . . . Assure me that I yet may change these shadows you have shown me, by an altered life!"

As he begged the Phantom for another chance, the specter's hood and dress become a bedpost. Scrooge realized he had been sleeping. He exclaims, "I will live in the Past, the Present, and the Future. The Spirits of all Three shall strive within me. Oh Jacob Marley! Heaven, and the Christmas Time be praised for this!"

And Dickens comments, "Best and happiest of all,

the time before him was his own, to make amends in!"[11]

This, I believe, closely approximates a Christian view of time. We were dead, but are now alive. All was lost, but—by grace—we've been given another chance.

The time we've been given in retirement is an opportunity to reflect such amazing grace to our neighbors, our co-workers, our families, and to the world. The days in retirement may seem long, but the years are short.

Let's all live like the redeemed Scrooge, overjoyed by the gift of time.

Chapter 6

Health

*Do you not know that your body is a temple of
the Holy Spirit within you, whom you have from
God? You are not your own, for you were bought
with a price. So glorify God in your body.*

1 Corinthians 6:19–20 ESV

"No limits. No labels. Aging is changing."

This motto from the AARP homepage speaks of "limitless" health in retirement. Eat between five to nine servings of fruit and vegetables each day, exercise daily to build cardiovascular health, stimulate "brain health" through mental exercise, meditate each day to relax, get eight to nine hours of sleep, and you too can have a healthy, happy, and limitless retirement.

Of course, these are all good health tips. But retirement also comes with daily reminders of our all-too-human limits. Shoulders ache. Wrinkles multiply. Trips to the doctor become more regular. Research tell us that it's likely that if you're older than 55, you likely have either hypertension or arthritis.[1] Not exactly debilitating, but not exactly "no limits," either.

This last spring, my mother and I took a vacation to Norway. Growing up a Minnesotan Scandinavian, she had always dreamed of visiting the land of our cultural heritage. (And we wanted to know if they said "Uff da" in Norway as much as we did in Minnesota.) So we booked the flights and headed for Norway. We ate on the streets of Oslo, visited the fish market in Bergen, kayaked a lake in Voss, and took a ferry through the majestic Nærøyfjord and Sognefjord. And my mom did great. At nearly 70, she hiked, adventured, and experienced a delightful, once-in-a life-time vacation.

But she was also recovering from a hip injury and slowed down for the second half of the trip. We sat at more cafés, rested, and observed the natural beauty of the Norwegian Fjords. The reminders of her humanity were subtle, but present. As we watched the ferries arrive in Flåm after a lunch, I was reminded that the body is not limitless. The body is mortal.

"I disagree with the 'disrupting aging' philosophy," says Dr. Hillary Lum, an assistant professor of Medicine-Geriatrics at the University of Colorado School of Medicine. "I strongly believe healthy aging includes recognition that we will not live forever, that we recognize loss, and that we need opportunities for connectedness and support. Choosing healthy behaviors is helpful," continues Lum, "but no easier to do as we age than in other times of life. Many seek healthy aging as an idol and may avoid relevant changes and opportunities to plan."[2]

Lum is part of a growing movement of physicians who are calling into question not just the ways we understand aging, but a medical establishment that suggests that nearly any physical problem can be solved with a pill, treatment, or technological solution.

If healthcare can be paid for (which is a significant fear for many entering retirement), the implicit message is to trust in the power of medical technology to keep our bodies healthy, happy, and young. Indeed, with $3.3 trillion in annual expenditures totaling 17.9 percent of total gross domestic product, the healthcare industry is enormously powerful.[3] Surely any broken body part can be fixed so that we can live a "limitless" life?

The biblical narrative has a very different view of the body. The body is good because God made it and God Himself took on a body while walking on earth. Yet it is also a "tent" that becomes frail and eventually dies (2 Cor. 5:1).

This willingness to see and even embrace our frailty has been popularized by books like Atul Gawande's *Being Mortal*, a beautiful yet painful look at aging in America. Even so, there still is a hesitancy to look squarely at bodies that age, deteriorate, and ultimately fail us. Fear—especially of dementia and losing one's independence later in life—still drives many medical decisions for those in retirement.

But I believe Christianity offers a more hopeful— and humbler—vision of the body. Our faith appreciates medicine, but does not place ultimate hope in doctors; it does not fear suffering, but faces suffering alongside a suffering Savior; and it sees our ultimate destiny not as disembodied souls, but as resurrected bodies in the new heavens and earth. And faith can give us insight for both healthcare decisions and healthy living as we pursue healthy, yet mortal, lives.

COMMON:

Fear of aging and losing one's independence drives many medical decisions for those in retirement.

vs.

UNCOMMON:

Christianity offers a more hopeful—and humbler—vision of the body.

THE POWER OF MEDICINE

In the past century, medicine has changed the West and the whole world. Harvard historian Niall Ferguson makes the case in *Civilization: The West and the Rest* that science was key to the West's global dominance in the last 500 years, especially with regard to healthcare. As scientists revealed the mysteries of the microbial world, doctors began to push back disease and illness as never before. Even in European colonies, often rife with injustice, life expectancy rose drastically. In French colonies, for example, life expectancy in Senegal grew from 30.2 years in 1945 to 52.3 in 2000; in Vietnam it grew from 22.5 years in 1930 to 69.4 in 2000; and it rose from 28.8 years in Tunisia in 1935 to 72.1 in 2000. Medicine and science were triumphant.[4]

Today, medicine is not just a service or profession, it's a powerful force. Over 13 million people work in healthcare, the federal government spends over $1 trillion each year on Medicare and Medicaid, and each year Americans spend an average of $10,348 on healthcare per person.[5] The medical establishment dominates human experience, from life's first cry until final breath.

But some physicians see cracks in medicine's promise to care for any and every need the body may have.

Abraham Nussbaum, a psychiatrist and author of *The Finest Traditions of My Callings: One Physician's Search for the Renewal of Medicine*, began residency as all doctors do: working on dead body parts. For Nussbaum, the autopsy was a metaphor for how medicine sees its live patients today. "Parts and money—too often that is what we physicians see when we look at patients," says Nussbaum. "What is broken? Can it be patched or does it need to be replaced? How much can I bill for the procedure?" Medicine has become efficient at "generating money by trying to fix faltering parts," says Nussbaum. Hearts, hips, and hairlines can all be fixed . . . for a price.[6]

But have we come to not just trust our doctors for medical care, but place our hope in them as the high priests of the body offering health (and salvation?) to all who place their faith in their powers?

Trust in Doctors, But Hope in God

"To place the hope of one's health in the hands of the doctor is the act of an irrational animal," wrote the fourth-century bishop St. Basil of Caesarea, founder of history's first public hospital for the poor. "This, nevertheless, is what we observe in the case of certain unhappy persons who do not hesitate to call their doctors their saviors. . . . When reason allows, we call in the doctor, but we do not leave off hoping in God."[7]

Basil's view of medicine was a balanced one. He believed it was "God's gift to us," an art given to mankind for healing the body, "since the body suffers affliction from both excess and deficiency" after the fall in the garden of Eden. Yet he also believed, "We must take great care to employ this medical art, if it should be necessary, not as making it wholly accountable for our state of health or illness, but as redounding to the glory of God."[8]

Basil offers a unique view to those hampered by intestinal pain or to those working as internists: health is a gift from God, not a possession to be purchased. Doctors are servants, not saviors. And bodies are not machines with interchangeable parts. Rather, bodies and souls are one intertwined holy place where God Himself dwells (1 Cor. 6:19).

We should trust doctors to heal our bodies as they are able. But our enduring hope is reserved for God alone.

Bob Cutillo, a physician at the Colorado Coalition for the Homeless, believes that medicine must accept its limits but the church also must own its failure.

"Modern medicine as well as the community that supports it have become confused about its purpose and transferred hope for salvation from the halls of faith to the corridors of medicine," says Cutillo. But the church has let this happen and accepted far too passive a role in conversations about health.

The church, however, has no reason to cower, says Cutillo:

> For the church knows the future in light of God's promises, sees the possibility for healing from the most unexpected places, and holds a view of the sick as members of a community who, by being loved and loving others, still have important roles to play despite being infirm and in bed.[9]

Faith and medicine can indeed work in cooperation. Each has valuable roles to play in God's world. Medicine can uniquely bridge the world of illness and health, train practitioners to be healers, and teach us to live in and through our bodies.

The church can help medicine grasp the idea of covenant. "The doctor-patient relationship thrives as a covenant of trust," says Cutillo, "but atrophies as a contract for purchased services." The church can offer medicine a vision of gratitude, for our bodies and our patients; it can elucidate the connection between body, soul, and prayer (James 5:14–15); and it can give medicine a vision for suffering and pain. "Rather than seeking to explain it or control it, the church can dwell in suffering without recoil," says Cutillo, "because in communion with a personal and present God who suffered with us, it believes in a redemptive promise that absorbs suffering."[10]

Though retirement may be too early to discuss old age, it's not too early to start healing our notions about health, the body, and suffering in light of the hope of glory.

RESTORING THE BODY— INCARNATION, DEATH, AND RESURRECTION

"Why does Great-Grandma's face wiggle, Mom?"

My 5-year-old daughter, Sierra, bluntly asked my wife this honest question about the hanging skin on Great-Grandma Dorothy's face. Glasses, white hair, and a wide smile full of her original teeth, Great-Grandma had long since passed the age of retirement. But Sierra's honesty made me think of the day when my face too will wiggle.

Only months after visiting Great-Grandma Dorothy, my wife, Kelly, my two daughters, and I visited Albert Lea, Minnesota, for the funeral of Great-Grandpa Russ. I still remember Sierra and Lily, huddling in a corner of a church stairwell, faces flush red with tears, saying, "Great-Grandpa is dead! Don't you understand? Dead!"

They felt a mix of sorrow and confusion. Great-Grandpa Russ was the happy man with a jolly belly who invited grandkids on his lap after Thanksgiving dinner. But now his *body* had changed. It had gone white and cold, lying in a coffin. And most noticeably, his stomach had shrunk considerably. Who was this person, my daughters thought, with a tiny tummy?

Both of these stories remind me not so much of retirement, but of the fact that our culture surrounding retirement tries so hard to forget. So much talk of healthy aging and medical solutions can't deny the final statistic: 100 percent of us die. And so many entertain and distract themselves with trips, movies, or golf, not wanting to recognize the inevitable. Often, we dance around conversations of our mortality, simply not knowing what to say. In doing so, we lose the chance to plan for a full life, whether in sickness or in health.

But I believe Christianity gives us a clear view of the body that allows us to face the realities of aging, as well as healthy living, with an unconquerable hope for retirement and beyond. Incarnation, crucifixion, and resurrection are the solid foundations for understanding our bodies.

The incarnation says that the body is good—and worth caring for.

"In the beginning was the Word, and the Word was with God, and the Word was God . . . . And the Word became flesh and dwelt among us" (John 1:1–14 ESV). God became a man, complete with sweat, hunger, taste buds, and tired feet. Such a thought was unthinkable to the Greek mind of the apostle John's day. The Greeks had a dualistic view of the material world. They believed the body was bad and the spirit (or the "Platonic forms") was good. Yet Christians insisted that Jesus was "clothed in flesh, the Godhead see; hail the incarnate Deity," as we sing at Christmas. All this "fleshiness" is something God planned for, approved of, and even lived in while on earth. And because of this, the body is deeply good. As Brian Wren's hymn puts it: the Word that has become flesh is good.[11]

Throughout Christian history, we've often co-opted the heresy that the body is bad and only the spirit is good.[12] Yet, the incarnation has always pointed to the fact that God cares deeply about our bodies. So much so, that He left the throne of heaven to become a fragile baby, susceptible to injury and pain, just like you and me.

This is a stark contrast from many attitudes around the body in contemporary retirement culture. For example, the 2017 film *Going Out in Style* features three retired friends who rob a bank after their pensions vanish. The comedy is a humorous look at aging, complete with a getaway in a three-wheeled mobility scooter; however, the underlying storyline still suggests the "I'm old, I deserve it" view of retirement. Retirement is the chance to finally get what you deserve. Though a bank heist film seems harmless, the more concerning side of this view of the body is found at The Villages in Florida, the 20,000-acre central Florida retirement community that has one of fastest growing rates of STDs in the country.[13] Here, pleasure reigns. Paul saw this same view of the body in his day: "Let us eat and drink, for tomorrow we die" (1 Cor. 15:32).

COMMON:

Retirement is the chance to finally get what you deserve.

vs.

UNCOMMON:

The body is the dwelling place of the Holy Spirit. We are to "honor God with [our] bodies" (1 Cor. 6:20).

But the incarnation says that the body is good and worth caring for because it is the dwelling place of the Holy Spirit. We are to "honor God with [our] bodies" (1 Cor. 6:20). Christians have a motivation to care for our bodies over a lifetime. For example, such practices include:

Exercise

Retired Air Force general and former president of the Navigators Jerry White played competitive handball several times a week through his sixties, seventies, and now early eighties. When I last met with him, he had his workout clothes on and seemed invigorated by the thought of his next match.

Relationships

George Vaillant's *Triumphs of Experience* tells the story of the decades-long Harvard Grant Study, the longest ever study of human development. After studying a group of men for over seventy-five years, Vaillant found the number one factor in living a long, healthy life for the men in the study was quality relationships. A single loving relative, mentor, or friend could actually cause longer life. Loving relationships were the key to longevity.[14]

Alcohol

Vaillant's study also found that alcoholism was the single greatest factor in causing divorces among men in the study. Alcohol caused stressors like bankruptcy and job loss that fractured relationships. "Alcoholism is a disorder of great destructive power,"[15] Vaillant writes. It also was a primary cause of depression later in life.

Food

True, it's not what we put in the body that makes us unclean but what comes out of the body (Matt. 15:11). Yet because Christians believe the body is the temple of the Holy Spirit, nutrition is an important factor in honoring God.

Aging

"Gray hair [is] the splendor of the old" (Prov. 20:29). As the body ages, the Bible gives us the view that aging is normal and even a reward for a righteous life (Prov. 16:31). It doesn't need to be avoided or "disrupted." Aging is a part of a full human life and can be embraced.

Sister Joan Chittister summarizes a Christian view of the body well: "Our moral obligation is to stay as well as we can, to remain active, to avoid abusing our bodies, to do the things that interest us and to enrich the lives of those around us."[16]

The death of Christ shows
that our bodies too will suffer—and Christ suffers with us.

Kerry Egan, author of *On Living,* had an emergency C-section with her first baby. During surgery, the epidural anesthesia failed. "I could feel everything, but the dangerous part was that I was moving while I was still cut open," Eagan remembers. So they gave her ketamine, a drug usually used only on the battlefield, with horses, or at raves (a party usually involving dancing, electronic music, and drug use). The drug induced a psychotic state, one that lasted for seven months.

Egan was a new mother but was plagued with hallucinations, delusions, and thoughts of suicide. She slept through nearly eighteen months on a mix of psychiatric medicines, having almost no memory of her son's first year and half of life. "I was deeply ashamed that I had lost my mind," said Egan.[17] She lost control of her body and felt the pang of shame.

We Americans, I believe, are ashamed of our suffering and dependence on others. Our ideals tell us the highest vision of a good life is independence and self-reliance. And so when we need medicine, prayer, or help to use the toilet after surgery, we feel shame. We hide our fragility.

At only 19 years old, I distinctly remember feeling this shame in my own life when I had surgery on both of my feet. When the doctors took off the bandages, I looked at my feet in horror. Green, blue, yellow, and swollen, with pins sticking out of each of my ten toes, I was confined to a wheelchair for months. *What good am I if I can't do anything?* I thought. I fell into a period of depression.

Suffering unmasks our true and deep dependence on others. It can lead us to recognize our place as dependent creatures, in need of others for every sip of water, every lumen of electricity, every meal we eat.

I've also seen that suffering can lead to either resentment or to humility. Suffering can stir up feelings of "I don't deserve this." Or it can lead us into the words of the psalmists who cry out in anguish, with the hope that God would hear us—we who are flesh, dust, and ashes—and be merciful.

Retirement is a season of possibility yet also of increased reminders of mortality. The cross of Christ does not "solve" the problem of suffering. (All attempts to solve the problem of evil have ended up like Job's friends who foolishly tried to solve it while their friend was suffering—something God chastised them for [Job 42:7].) But it does mean that we need not avoid or look away from suffering because Christ is present in the tears and anguish of His people.

He is not only the King of glory, but He is also a Man of sorrows (Isa. 53:3).

The resurrection of Christ means our bodies too will be resurrected in a world without end.

What will life be like after death? This question has spurred hundreds of heaven books and hospital-room testimonials. It has also been the primary question for evangelical churches in the twentieth century, hoping to "save" as many as possible.

But the real question, according to theologian and author N.T. Wright, is: What will *life* after life after death be like?

Wright's voluminous scholarship has challenged the prevailing idea that the Christian's ultimate destiny after death is a disembodied state in a purely spiritual existence in heaven. Wright says this is *not* what the Easter story is primarily about. Easter morning points to the physical, bodily resurrection of Christ. Wright believes the gospels *aren't primarily about going to heaven after you die.* The emphasis of Christian hope is that "Jesus's resurrection is the beginning of God's new project not to snatch people away from earth to heaven, but to colonize earth with the life of heaven."[18]

The early church built this into its most well-known creed: "We believe in the resurrection of the body and the life of the world to come." This belief drove Christians to care deeply for the bodies of those in the Roman Empire like, for example, those who were dying from the plague. It was the hope of resurrection, says Rodney Stark in *The Rise of Christianity*, that led Christians to care for the ill, even though they risked perishing in the process.[19]

What does this mean for the body in retirement? What practical value does the doctrine of the resurrection have for our lives now, as we consider how to spend our retirement?

After Paul explains the centrality of the resurrection to

Christian faith in 1 Corinthians 15, he concludes, "Always give yourselves fully to the work of the Lord, because you know your labor in the Lord is not in vain" (v. 58). What's the connection between resurrection and our work?

Apparently, God cares about our bodies so much, *all the labor we do in the name of Christ to serve other bodies*—sitting with a sick friend, clipping the toenails of an ungrateful mother-in-law, cleaning a grandchild's dirty dishes—points to God's new creation. It is not just the next world that matters, but Christ loves *this* world (John 3:16). If God will renew our bodies as heaven one day comes to earth, our work in this age is a signpost and a symbol of the glory to come.

The gist of it: Paul says that since your body will be resurrected, get to work. Though mortal, because of God's victory at Calvary, you have nothing to fear.

Christ has died. Christ is risen. Christ will come again.

Chapter 7

Learning

The beginning of wisdom is this: Get wisdom.
Though it cost all you have, get understanding.

Proverbs 4:7

"The crowning grace of old age is influence," wrote
Cicero, the great Roman statesmen. He believed long-
lasting influence was the result of deep character and a
nimble mind.

Cicero walked the talk. At 84 years old, nearly two
decades past our current age of retirement, he described
how he spent his days.

> I am now engaged in composing the seventh book
> of my *Origins*. I collect all the records of antiquity
> . . . I am writing treatises on augural, pontifical, and
> civil law. I am, besides, studying hard at Greek,
> and after the manner of the Pythagoreans—to keep
> my memory in working order—I repeat in the eve-
> ning whatever I have said, heard, or done during

the day. These are the exercises of the intellect, these the training grounds of the mind.[1]

Cicero regularly attended the Senate, appeared in court on behalf of his friends, and found unending delight in "the garden and the orchard, the feeding of sheep, the swarms of bees, endless varieties of flowers."[2] His days were filled with gardening, study, writing, public debate, and a lifelong love of learning.

Yet two thousand years later, the image of learning later in life has morphed from acquiring wisdom and influencing the public sphere to pursuing "brain fitness" to prevent memory loss and taking enrichment classes for seniors.

Today, "brain fitness" is all the rage. John Medina's *Brain Rules for Aging Well* shows that healthy eating, exercise, and even brain-training video games can change the structure of your brain and slow down aging. And Norman Doidge, author of *The Brain That Changes Itself,* is finding that the brain is "plastic" and can change its structure into old age. Some practices may potentially even *reverse* the effects of Alzheimer's disease.[3]

Today there are more opportunities than ever for formal and informal education in your fifties, sixties, and beyond. You could become a Road Scholar and take educational trips featuring on-site lectures from New Zealand to Washington D.C. to France.[4] If those are out of your price range, there are Osher Lifelong Learning Institutes on college campuses around the country offering non-credit, affordable classes ranging from Chinese culture to American music history. Retirement communities often follow suit with classes of their own, offering classes on everything from photography to bird watching.

Blossoming opportunities to learn long into retirement are one of the blessings of the information age. Yet if we take a step back and look at perspectives on learning in retirement, we might wonder: What are the underlying *motives* behind learning later in life present in our culture today?

WHAT DRIVES OUR LEARNING?

First, might the brain fitness craze actually be masking a deep fear? *What if I become one of the 5.7 million Americans with Alzheimer's disease? What if I become a burden to my kids? What if my mind betrays me in my eighties—or even earlier?* Many would do anything to prevent that dark future.

Second, has learning simply become a form of entertainment, a way to "occupy" your time in retirement? In many senior learning contexts, we might question whether learning has become more about consuming information, rather than about influencing the public through wisdom in old age.

Third, we underestimate how difficult it is in retirement to reengage the world of learning after a career. Often our careers narrow our horizons. We become good at a single thing, like processing mortgages or wiring electrical. Consequently, it becomes difficult to broaden our perspective simply because a lifetime of work has been focused on a single skill or talent, rather than on broadly engaging the world beyond our home or workplace.

Developing a desire for reading classics, taking college classes, or researching space travel requires flexing new muscles in retirement. Acquiring new habits of learning in retirement can be *difficult,* a challenge vastly underestimated by many well-meaning educators. Learning in retirement requires not only curiosity but *courage*—the courage to admit areas of ignorance, submit yourself to a course of study, and become a student once more.

As an adult, I learned Spanish . . . or tried to. When my wife and I spent a year in Ecuador, we found that one of the most difficult things to do when learning a foreign language was having a dinner conversation with a native speaker. Conversations would start, and then stop, before we could jump in. At one such dinner, I wanted to stand up and say, "Slow down! I'm still conjugating the preterite form of *conocer,* here!" Instead, we just smiled and ate our enchiladas, pretending like we knew what everybody was saying.

The people who were most helpful to Kelly and me in learning a new language in Ecuador were actually children—preferably age five or six. They spoke slowly. They used simple language. They were *patient* with us. (And they smiled lots at the tall white people with clumsy words.) After our year in Ecuador, I looked back and realized that I felt a little silly to have my vocabulary reduced to that of a kindergartener for a year. But we also realized that a serving of humble pie is often necessary to becoming an effective learner.

Though this kind of humility is difficult to muster at any age, many find the courage to learn and explore new horizons in retirement.

Verona Mullison, 65, is a Cru missionary (formerly Campus Crusade for Christ) and is now considering how to use her next season of life. When she was in her 20s, she worked in a hospital lab. Originally, she went with Cru to be a medical missionary but then spent years at home with her kids while on the mission field. Now, however, as she considers her retirement, her old love of science has been rejuvenated. She's studied neuroplasticity for fun and taught our (young) staff at Denver Institute for Faith & Work about Norman Doidge's research.

Verona speaks excitedly about retirement. "I am looking forward to feeding my desire for learning, which I've had since I was a kid." For Verona, retirement is a chance to pick up on the unexplored strands of curiosity in her life—such as the sciences—that she's always wanted to learn about but hasn't had the time to explore. And for Verona, learning in retirement is connected to her sense of calling. She wants to grow not just in knowledge but in wisdom.

WISDOM IS AS WISDOM DOES

Christian learning has its basis in the Great Commandment: "Love the Lord your God with all your heart and with all your soul and with all your strength and with all your *mind*," writes Luke the physician, and "Love your neighbor as yourself" (Luke 10:27). Rather than the mere accumulation of information, the pursuit of wisdom begins with turning your eyes to God Himself, and culminates with taking meaningful action on behalf of your neighbors.

The ancient Greeks loved ideas for ideas' sake, but the Jews thought this was silly. Luke writes (perhaps sarcastically?) in the book of Acts, "All the Athenians and the foreigners who lived there spent their time doing nothing but talking about and listening to the latest ideas" (Acts 17:21). Reason was prized by the Jews, but to become wisdom, it needed to be tied to morality. Jesus Himself made this point when He said that wisdom is proved right by her actions (Luke 7:35). His half-brother James echoes Jesus' words: "Who among you is wise and understanding? Let him show by his good behavior his deeds in the gentleness of wisdom" (James 3:13 NASB).

Who we become is more important than what we know. Yet learning and character are connected, like a book and its cover. If character is the pages, learning is the binding.

The first time I met Vernon Grounds, he was 92 years old, the founder and then chancellor of Denver Seminary. During my seminary experience, I had wanted to hear from the living legend who rubbed shoulders with some of the leading voices in twentieth-century Christianity, like Francis Schaeffer and Billy Graham. As a

> ## COMMON:
> **What we know is more important than who we become.**
>
> ### vs.
>
> ## UNCOMMON:
> **Who we become is more important than what we know.**

psychologist, theologian, and social reformer, Grounds retired in 1979, yet was appointed as the chancellor in 1993, where he continued to hold weekly office hours until just before his death.

I walked into his voluminous personal library for our appointment. As a nervous 26-year-old, I sat in the presence of this short, kind, and gentle man, spectacles resting on his nose. He had an unmistakable spiritual aura about him. As I took a seat in his office, I asked him the secret to his long, fruitful life. After mentioning his love of learning and enjoyment of his work, he said, "It's you! Being around young seminarians and learning from you keeps me young." His delight in learning fused with a love for people and became Christlike character.

Vernon Grounds became a person of deep wisdom and long-lasting influence. The question for us to consider, then, is how might retirement be a time to cultivate both deep learning *and* deep character?

Scripture suggests it starts not with a book, but with a community.

Choose the right community.

In my years after graduate school, I came to value the primacy of learning from *people*: people who were further along in their careers, people with different training than my own, people from different ethnic or social backgrounds. As I grew in my career, I saw myself imitating leaders I knew and putting into practice what they were *feeling and doing* far before I understood the *concepts* behind their actions. I've come to believe it's the people with whom we live in close community who most form our hearts, minds, and souls. "Walk with the wise and become wise, for a companion of fools suffers harm" (Prov. 13:20).

Years ago, I designed a program called the 5280 Fellowship, a nine-month intensive experience for young professionals on theology, work, and culture. Rather than it being text heavy, I designed it around how I believe character is formed, not just how brains take in information.[5] First, people are most often formed in contexts of pain or struggle. Character is fused in the crucible of suffering, not generally the ease of luxury. But second, it's the high-commitment communities you join, and their shared stories and habits, which are most formative.

The question for people reading a book (like this one) then is not, what will I read next, but *with whom* will I learn? This might be enrolling in an undergraduate course of studies, it might be joining a church small group, or it might be committing to a senior leadership program. The choice of who you spend your time with will determine more of your character than just what you read.

Connect learning to your calling and work.

Oftentimes, learning is a sheer delight. Discovering the way a coral reef feeds tropical fish, or how to perfectly prune a rosebush, carries its own reward. Other times learning is a means of exploration. Like the Europeans who encountered the "new world" in the fifteenth and sixteenth centuries, learning can be an adventure of discovery.

Yet many times, like in Verona's story, retirement is the chance to pick up the strands of your calling that might have been latent during your career and develop them more fully into your life's work.

Kent Johnson was overflowing with ideas. When we met for lunch, I could barely get a word in—and I was better off for it. During lunch near the Colorado state capitol, he bubbled with enthusiasm for his next challenge.

For thirty years, Kent served as senior counsel at Texas Instruments, and during his career as a lawyer he noticed how Christians are often stereotyped in the workplace. So he decided to start a consulting practice called Religious Diversity at Work, which helps companies and other organizations connect with diverse religious workforces, moving them "beyond mere 'tolerance' and toward mutually respectful, deeply caring relationships."[6]

As a religious diversity consultant, Kent now works

with corporations to help them include, rather than exclude, diverse perspectives in the workplace. At a conference hosted by leaders in the LGBT community, Kent was invited to speak because of a relationship of trust he had developed with the organizer. In a breakout session, attendees were shocked to learn that Christianity was a faith built on love and not hate. Kent's calling in the next season of life is to be a bridge between people who often know very little about one another.

Kent, like many baby boomers, is taking "retirement" to mean "refocus" on the issues and topics he cares about most deeply. With twenty or even thirty years of work ahead of him, learning in retirement can be preparation for a new job, career, or volunteer position that flows from a God-given calling.

Learn to serve.

Why would anybody spend their golden years reading ancient history, speaking in the Senate, publishing books, and otherwise influencing their communities? Why not take it easy and step back from public life? As Cicero asked these questions with his own friends, he concluded that the "illustrious" souls of human history "would [not] have attempted such lofty deeds as to be remembered by posterity, had they not seen in their minds that future ages concerned them."[7] Great people care not just about themselves but about future generations.

Dietrich Bonhoeffer, German pastor and martyr, said something similar in the dark days of World War II. He made the risky move to take part in a plot to assassinate

Hitler—one that ultimately cost him his life—out of a similar conviction. "The ultimately responsible question is not how I extricate myself heroically from a situation," Bonhoeffer wrote in *Letters and Papers from Prison,* "but how a coming generation is to go on living."[8]

Yet today, this removal from society is exactly how our culture frames retirement: How will you extricate yourself from the world and live a healthy, happy, care-free life?

Bonhoeffer believed that love *compelled* him to get involved, to engage, and to serve, even in the most difficult of circumstances. He believed his actions could have a generational impact. Rather than retreating, he took responsibility for the course of future generations.

Václav Havel was a playwright, philosopher, and the first president of the Czech Republic after communism was toppled in the former Soviet Union. He had a similar perspective to both Bonhoeffer and Cicero. He once said,

> Whenever I have encountered any kind of deep problem with civilization anywhere in the world—be it the logging of rain forests, ethnic or religious intolerance or the brutal destruction of a cultural landscape that has taken centuries to develop—somewhere at the end of the long chain of events that gave rise to the problem at issue I have always found one and the same cause: a lack of accountability to and responsibility for the world.[9]

Havel was motivated not just by defending his rights, but by his responsibility and sense of duty to his countrymen.

What if our motive for learning in retirement was taking responsibility for the well-being of our communities and the world that God so loves (John 3:16)?

For Christians, learning is a category of love. Christians ask how they might learn in order to *give:* to their work, their family, their local church, their communities, their culture, and to future generations. Christians are not driven by the fear of memory loss or old age, because fear is not a Christian habit of mind (1 John 4:18). They do not hoard knowledge or learn as a means to superiority over others, because "'knowledge' puffs up, but love builds up" (1 Cor. 8:1 ESV). Instead, Christians are motivated to learn out of a love for God and a love for their neighbors. Even in old age they refuse to retreat from the world because the resurrection gives them hope not only for the next world but for *this one.* They give to their neighbors the knowledge, experience, and wisdom that has been uniquely entrusted to them.

John Milton once wrote, "The end then of learning is to repair the ruins of our first parents by [seeking] to know God aright."[10] Christian learning begins with understanding God's great love for us. Yet through our vocations, it culminates in the healing of God's broken world.

Chapter 8

Mentoring

*One generation commends your works
to another; they tell of your mighty acts.*

Psalm 145:4

My experience of mentoring began with two disasters.

As a young seminary student, one of our graduation requirements was to find two mentors. One mentor quit on me after three months. Though he made a three-year commitment, his abruptness made it clear: our relationship was transactional. I felt like a wet dog in the rain.

My other mentor, a kind-hearted counselor, stuck it out, but the relationship simply felt awkward. Our coffee dates always felt like he was supposed to show up with nuggets of wisdom, and I was supposed make a profound life application before my latte was finished. When my degree program ended, so did our relationship. We never found enough common ground to build something more than checking off an "I'm-supposed-to-do-this" box.

But I've also had incredibly fruitful mentoring experiences.

Earlier this year we invited John Marsh, an entrepreneur from Opelika, Alabama, to speak at one of our events at Denver Institute for Faith & Work. After the event, I headed to a pub near the Denver Center for the Performing Arts with Pete Ochs, a business leader from Kansas, and John, one of our 5280 Fellows. I sat next to John, whose graying hair, blue-framed glasses, and a sleek suit coat seemed to accentuate his energy during our conversation.

John's enthusiasm for business, his talent for marketing, and his philosophy of renewing small towns were contagious. After only thirty minutes, I could tell his disarming southern drawl was buttressed by an incredibly sharp intellect and deep personal humility. He told me, "Jeff, I've been all over the country speaking to faith and work conferences. And yours was the best I've ever seen. How come nobody's heard of you guys?"

At first blush, I wondered if he was joking. Did he really mean we were the *best?* I wasn't sure. Second, I heard a challenge. Why *hadn't* we expanded our reach further? John both affirmed and challenged me—signs of a master mentor.

That night, I took John back to his hotel after a film screening in Boulder. In the car, we talked about our shared love of entrepreneurship. John has over a dozen businesses. I asked him how he could get all of his work done. He said, "Jeff, each of my businesses can only take a few hours of me per week!"

As an entrepreneur with a thousand ideas myself—and a personality that people often tell me can be intimidating—when he said that, I immediately felt like there was *another me* in the world. The ancient philosophers said that a true friend was "another self." C. S. Lewis picked up on this idea and said friendship was not built on looking *at* each other, like romantic love, but instead was forged by standing side by side, engrossed in some common interest.[1] I felt that John and I saw the world as one big opportunity, and our ideas could be both a blessing and sometimes exhausting.

Weeks later I took two of my colleagues to visit John in Alabama to seek his advice on a new learning platform we were building. Since then, we've scheduled a mentoring call every other week. Quickly, John became for me a trusted guide. And he opened the door through delight, affirmation, and an invitation to relationship.

I asked John in one of our first mentoring phone calls, "What makes for an effective mentoring relationship?" He replied, "It has to be two ways. Both sides have to add value to each other or it never works out." As the months have developed, John gives me his on-the-ground insight into entrepreneurship and city-building. I return the favor with sharing what I know about theology, work, and culture. We both give, and we both receive.

For me, John is not just a mentor. He's a friend.

FROM MENTORSHIP TO INTERGENERATIONAL FRIENDSHIP

Mentoring in retirement sounds like a wonderful idea. "Invest in the next generation. Share your life experience. Feel a renewed sense of purpose." But in reality, far too often mentoring feels awkward for both mentor and mentee.

To the mentee, it can often feel like a monodirectional exchange of information, the older imparting "wisdom" to the younger during weekly or monthly appointments. Interactions are often confined to stiff formality and contrived "coffee chats" in which a mentor is supposed to (halo glowing) grace the young Padawan with Yoda-like insight. Anxiety bubbles under the surface for the mentee: Will I be heard in this meeting, or just get "should upon" for the next hour?

To the mentor, the high expectations surrounding mentoring can create a sense of pressure and a feeling of inadequacy that deters people from mentoring in the first place. Doubts creep in. *Do I really have something to share with the next generation? Would they want to listen?*

Today many are swapping a traditional idea of mentoring for the practice of *intergenerational friendship.* Steven Strott, a consultant with the Boston Consulting Group in his early thirties, explains, "Rather than a transfer of wisdom from an august elder to an unseasoned youth, mentorship should be supplemented with the idea of *intergenerational friendship,* a relationship that flourishes across an age gap, to the mutual enrichment of the younger *and* the older."[2]

Steven has experienced the benefits of an intergenerational friendship firsthand. Steven met Barry and Linda Rowan at business school, though their respective graduations were separated by three decades. After Barry and Linda led a microfinance trip to Central America for business school alumni, they struck up a mutual friendship with Steven. During snowshoe trips to the mountains, Steven would share reflections from Scripture. Barry would reciprocate with insights from his last spiritual retreat. Over a number of years, they shared brownie recipes, Excel spreadsheet formulas (both Barry and Steven are MBAs in finance), prayer requests, and eventually the same employer. As time passed, Steven realized Barry and Linda had helped him make professional decisions, navigate relationships, and grow spiritually. Barry and Linda had become Steven's mentors, but their relationship looked—and felt—a lot more like friendship.

Though "mentorship" didn't fully enter our common vocabulary until the 1970s and 1980s, the idea has its roots in Homer's *Odyssey*, written in the eighth century BC. While Odysseus is at war, his son, Telemachus, is cared for by Mentor. The goddess Athena appears to Telemachus in the form of Mentor to offer divine wisdom, guidance, and advice. Perhaps it's just this kind of divine guidance that's expected of mentors today that makes the idea of mentoring so off-putting, especially to people who know their personal and professional flaws all too well.

For Christians who are both indwelt by the Holy Spirit and are brothers and sisters in Christ, the idea of intergenerational friendship finds a natural home. As Jesus explained to His disciples, "I no longer call you servants. . . . Instead, I have called you friends" (John 15:15). Surely, this must have been a stunning statement to receive from One who had raised Lazarus, fed 5,000 people, and healed the blind. But for Christians, older and younger are sons and daughters of the same Father. For Christ followers, there is never a reason to feel superior to others, because we are all sinners saved by God's grace; yet there is never a reason to feel inferior, either, for we all made in God's image and adorned with eternal worth.

The countercultural nature of the gospel shows us that blessing flows not only from wise to naïve, but also from the foolish back to the wise (1 Cor. 1:27). Such is the nature of God's upside-down kingdom, where we become strong through weakness, we gain riches through giving them away, the first are the last, and the servants are the greatest. Christians have a natural starting point to begin a relationship of mentoring—a common affection for Jesus. Yet they do so out of a posture of humility, knowing that both older and younger have much to give, and have much to receive.

In the Bible, "mentoring" relationships between older and younger flourished. Paul mentored Timothy, Samuel mentored Saul and David, Elijah mentored Elisha, Mordecai mentored Esther, and Priscilla and Aquila mentored Apollos. But in each case, the wisdom came from fixing one's eyes first on God, not only on the sage. And the giving was often mutual. We wouldn't cite Paul's influence on Timothy's life if Timothy hadn't also served alongside Paul (Rom. 16:21).

The stories that get mentoring right all point to this mutuality. In the 2000 film *Finding Forrester*, William Forrester (Sean Connery) and Jamal Wallace (Rob Brown) strike up an unlikely friendship around their common love of books and writing. Forrester, a "retired" writer, helps Wallace find his voice and navigate a new school; Wallace, an African-American teenager, helps Forrester confront his fears of the world outside of his apartment. Each gave. Each received.

There are few things so human and so cross-cultural as the older grandparent, parent, boss, or teacher sharing insight and life experience with the grandchild, child, employee, or student. But I've found the entry point into a mentoring relationship makes all the difference.

How Mentoring Actually Works

"There are certain things that happen uniquely in Christian institutions of education that make a profound difference in your likelihood to succeed," says Michael Lindsay, president of Gordon College, about his research on elite leaders. "Principally, it's about having a formative relationship with a mentor."

In Lindsay's research on people who achieved high levels of leadership in business, government, and the nonprofit sector, he found that a connection to a mentor early in one's career was the single most important factor in career success. Lindsay also found that lots of business schools and churches see this opportunity and try to create structured mentoring programs, but don't have much luck. For example, a management trainee is matched up with a senior executive, or adult mentors in a church are paired up with young people for Bible study. "Those are all well and good," says Lindsay, "but actually those don't work very effectively."

"The real way in which mentoring works effectively is through organic relationships," says Lindsay, "One of the most important things that Christian institutions can do is create the ecosystem of opportunity out of which those relationships can develop."[3]

Though pairing up mentors and mentees for monthly appointments usually falters, organizations that provide the *context* for those relationships to form can become very successful. For example, a two-week backpacking trip for recently retired engineers and early career engineers can create the environment out of which genuine friendships form. Early career fellowship programs, like the White House Fellowship, function on this model as well. Senior leaders meet regularly with Fellows for lunch to share about their career experiences and challenges for honest, off-the-record lunch conversations. These shared, intergenerational experiences are the black soil in which mentoring relationships grow and change lives.

I've found skilled mentors often share five characteristics.

1. Skilled mentors find genuine delight in the next generation and develop friendship based on common interests.

It might be baseball, city government, or philosophy. But rather than starting a mentoring relationship with a "you need this" mentality, talented mentors often develop the relationship because they're actually curious about the young person, want to learn alongside them, and share a common interest. This kind of humility cracks open the door for learning to be mutual and shared, rather than one way. This mutuality builds the trust necessary for not just skill transfer but spiritual formation to take place.

2. Skilled mentors bless and affirm a younger generation.

Rather than pointing out deficiencies, elders who become effective mentors are first people of wisdom and blessing.

For example, in Clint Eastwood's film *Gran Torino,* Walt Kowalski, a hardened, cursing, and angry Korean War veteran, ends up mentoring Thao, a Hmong teenager in Detroit who tried to steal Walt's car. Out of shame for his offense, Thao's family makes him do yard work for Kowalski for two weeks.

During those two weeks as Thao does chores for Kowalski, Kowalski enters Thao's world by eating food with his family, showing him his garage full of tools, and by encouraging him to date "Miss Yum Yum," a Hmong teenager that Thao struggles to even make eye contact with. Kowalski affirms the confidence-less Thao and even lets Thoa borrow his precious 1972 Gran Torino to bring his girlfriend to the movies.

Thao—like so many mentees—didn't first need advice. Rather, he needed to know he was valuable and had something unique to offer the world. He needed an elder to affirm his identity and point out his unique talents and value.

3. Skilled mentors share their stories and are genuinely vulnerable with their mentees.

The truth is, young people want to hear more about your mistakes than your successes. Having done hundreds of panel presentations for my work, I've found that vulnerability always goes way further than expertise. Advice is fine—when asked for. But hearing honest stories allows mentees to learn from a mentor's mistakes and, hopefully, not repeat them.

> ## COMMON:
> **Young people need your advice.**
>
> ### vs.
>
> ## UNCOMMON:
> **Young people want to hear more about your mistakes than your successes.**

Psychologists who study friendship find there's actually a fairly predictable formula to turning an acquaintance into a friend, including an intergenerational friend. It's this: self-disclosure + reciprocity = intimacy. So, if you gradually increase what you share with a friend over time, including negative emotions and stories of failure, and your friend reciprocates, you're on the path to intimacy.[4]

If great mentors are really just great intergenerational friends, the foundation of great mentoring is being willing to hold together both authority and vulnerability.[5]

4. Skilled mentors are patient and commit to long-term relationships.

Again, Michael Lindsay says, "What *does* matter [for the success of young adults] is the formative influence of an adult who speaks into your life and who has a sustaining relationship that you carry with you."[6] If each of us thinks of the people who've deeply influenced our lives, these are generally people we've known not for weeks or months, but for years. And they've endured our silliness, our sin, our mistakes— and are still there for us.

5. Skilled mentors ask more questions than they give answers.

Jesus Himself was master of the penetrating question. Questions like "What do you want me to do for you?" made Jesus' disciples stare into their own souls, and ask themselves what they truly desired. Of course, Jesus gave answers too. But genuine spiritual formation requires introspection, reflection, and prayer that is often the fruit of the right question at the right time.

Mentoring and the Opportunity Gap

Harvard sociologist Robert Putnam shows a disconcerting truth about America in the last fifty years: in nearly every social and economic category, life for the working class has deteriorated. For example, wages for high school educated men have dropped 47 percent. The rate of single-parent homes has jumped for working-class kids from 20 to 70 percent. And the educational gap between kids of working-class parents and professional parents is actually widening. Shockingly, high-achieving poor kids are now *less* likely to go to college than low-achieving rich kids. That is, smart poor kids have a *smaller* chance of getting a college degree than dumb rich kids. This "fact is particularly hard to square," Putnam writes, "with the idea at the heart of the American Dream: equality of opportunity."[7]

Seeing this widening gap between professionals and the working class, Putnam adds, "If America's religious communities were to become seized of the immorality of the opportunity gap, mentoring is one of the ways in which they could make an immediate impact."[8]

There are many opportunities to mentor in retirement — through a local school or civic programs like the Experience Corps. But I believe there is unique value to mentoring through a local church.

Sociologists say church involvement is associated with a wide host of benefits for both children and adults. Kids who go to church have higher academic achievement, better relationships with parents, and are more involved in extracurricular activities. Church-goers commit fewer crimes, are in better health, live longer, and make more money.[9]

Churches are a source of valuable relationships for working-class kids who tend to have fewer relational networks than their professional peers. If you're out of work, a used car from a church member might be a life-line. If your parents are never home, a retired mentor from your church could be your ticket to navigating the college admission process.

What if the 87 percent of baby boomers who believe in God decided that a central way they were going to spend their retirement was by mentoring young people through their local church? What if America's retirees traded comfort for purpose, and swapped retirement villages for communities of intergenerational friendship?

What if retirement became a source of renewed purpose for older Americans who decided to share their lives especially with young adults who needed their affirmation, delight, vulnerability, and patience?

What would it look like for you to develop a genuine intergenerational friendship with just one young person in your neighborhood?

"It is more blessed to give than to receive," said Jesus (Acts 20:35). But Jesus also says that it's not knowledge but action that brings the blessing.

"Now that you know these things, you will be blessed if you do them" (John 13:17).

Chapter 9

Family

"He commanded our ancestors to teach their children, so the next generation would know them, even the children yet to be born, and they in turn would tell their children. Then they would put their trust in God and would not forget his deeds but would keep his commands."

Psalm 78:5–7

"So why did you move to Denver?" As a fundraiser who meets dozens of baby boomers moving to my hometown each year, I frequently ask this question. And the vast majority of them answer the same things: "To be close to kids and grandkids."

Older adults report that the best part of retirement by far is being able to spend more time with family members. When asked about a wide range of potential benefits to growing older, seven in ten respondents age

65 and older said they look forward to spending more time with family.[1]

In interviews for this book, stories of family abounded: grandparents who delight in piano practices, soccer tournaments, and weekly babysitting routines; parents of adult children who help their kids get launched in their careers or buy their first home; and siblings who finally make that trip to North Dakota to catch up now that the grind of a career has subsided.

Reconnecting with family is a genuine joy of retirement. And for many, serving kids, grandkids, and aging parents is central to a sense of vocation in this season of life.

Yet family life in retirement is not all blissful cookouts on Sunday afternoon with three generations playing in the backyard. Tensions with family are just as real.

Supporting Adult Children. A 2011 study found that 70 percent of retirees expect their adult children will need financial assistance.[2] And a 2015 Pew Research survey of 1,500 adults in Germany, Italy, and the US found that over half had provided financial assistance to adult children over age 18.[3] In the past fifty years, "emerging adulthood"—the phase between adolescence and a full-fledged adulthood—has extended the amount of time many parents provide financially for their children.

Caring for Elderly Parents. The high cost of assisted living, memory care, and other healthcare costs for aging parents can exacerbate already-stressed retirement budgets. Those in their fifties and sometimes early sixties have been called a "sandwich generation" because they find themselves needing to provide for both children and parents at the same time. For example, Bryan Chrisman retired from his work as the president of National Christian Foundation Colorado to help care for his wife's aging mother in Kitty Hawk, North Carolina. "We just felt like it was the right thing to do. We wanted to 'honor your father and mother,'" he says. "And so we moved." Yet Bryan balances the needs of his grown children as they navigate post-college life with the needs of his mother-in-law; his work aspirations are tempered by his family's needs.

Caring for Grandchildren. Many grandparents find a deep joy in caring for their grandkids. But babysitting constantly can sometimes feel like you're giving free labor. (With four young kids ourselves, my wife and I have been guilty of presuming on my mother's generosity more than once.)

Tensions in Marriage. The divorce rate among US adults 50 and over has roughly doubled since the 1990s.[4] The phenomenon known as "gray divorce" is growing. Rob Pascale and Dr. Louis H. Primavera, co-authors of *The Retirement Maze: What You Should Know Before and After You Retire,* say, "Some couples might find they don't have quite as much in common as they once thought. While still in the workforce, underlying differences can be masked, because so much attention is taken up by work and raising a family. But these differences can come to the forefront when couples are more focused just on each other."[5] They found that after a honeymoon period, many couples grapple with the challenges of living in close proximity with each other, day-after-day, for the first time in decades—or for some, ever. Though many couples in retirement experience greater marital satisfaction, retirement often introduces new phase of negotiating schedules, finances, and family values.

Because of these increased family commitments in retirement, it's no wonder that retired men and women often find themselves wondering where all their "free time" went.

INTERGENERATIONAL LIVING

The combination of financial concerns and the desire to be close to extended family is leading more people to consider intergenerational living.

Greg Gast is the not-so-retired VP of Human Resources at Hudson River HealthCare, Inc. in Peekskill, New York. Greg and his wife, Nancy, decided to make a bold move and experiment with sharing a house with their oldest daughter, her husband, and their three kids. Greg and Nancy take the second floor of the 5,000-square-foot house, while their kids and grandkids take the basement, leaving the main floor as a common area.

Greg says there are distinct advantages to sharing a home: they share the same cable bill, lawn mower, and coffee pot. Sharing a mortgage also helps their budget and their daughter's budget. But there are also challenges: privacy and the occasional interpersonal clashes rise to the surface. "We've gotten better at communication," Gast says about their relationship with their daughter and son-in-law. "It's greatly helped to define our boundaries."

Mark Galli, the editor in chief of *Christianity Today*, says, "The church of our generation should be encouraging the children of boomers to invite their parents to live with them." Galli believes intergenerational living, though not always easy, is an opportunity for the American church to express love and honor toward retiring parents, many of whom are facing unexpected financial challenges.

Today conversations about intergenerational living are also extending beyond housing arrangements to the design of community. Jenks West Elementary School in Jenks, Oklahoma, has started programs such as Book Buddies, where students read to the "grandmas and grandpas," local seniors in the community.

Donna Butts, the executive director of Generations United, said about programs like those at Jenks West Elementary, "We have an aging population, and what we can't afford to do is set them in a Sun City-type arrangement so they're only sharing their experience and knowledge with other older adults."[6] While these intergenerational community arrangements aren't common, one study found that the number of "intergenerational shared sites"—such as a retirement community and preschool being next door—is growing, and is an asset both to seniors and to children.[7]

As finances pinch more Americans in retirement, more are choosing intergenerational options. One Pew Research study found that a surprising 26.9 million

Americans live in a three-generational home.[8] As this trend grows, so do the questions surrounding how to make multigenerational relationships work.

FAMILY—FOR BETTER OR FOR WORSE

The financial crunch of retirement is causing more boomers to ask how far their responsibilities extend to family . . . and how far their kids' responsibility extends to them as they age.

Christians often cite the fifth commandment in conversations about family responsibilities: "Honor your father and you mother, so that you may live long in the land the LORD your God is giving you" (Ex. 20:12). Parents deserve our respect and our care as they age. Paul deepens this expectation as he writes to Timothy about the need to provide for one's own household: "Anyone who does not provide for their relatives, and especially for their own household, has denied the faith and is worse than an unbeliever" (1 Tim. 5:8). Most people see providing for both parents and children as a responsibility.[9] Yet how, one might ask, might a believer care for a spouse, aging parents, adult children, and grandchildren—all on a shrinking retirement income that needs to last for decades?[10]

The reality is that tough decisions need to be made, and hard, open conversations are often difficult to have with family members. But with proper planning and boundary-setting, relationships with parents, kids, and grandkids can flourish in retirement.

Making a Plan

How should you think about family as you enter retirement? You can start here:

Set boundaries

Henry Cloud and John Townsend's classic book *Boundaries* reminds us that setting proper boundaries is key to healthy relationships. It's also important to define boundaries with family members early in retirement.

Some questions I suggest to consider include:

- To what extent will I financially support adult children? Have my spouse and I discussed this together? Have I been clear with my adult children on this topic?
- What does it mean to "honor your father and mother" as I walk through questions of age, illness, assisted living, and end-of-life care with my parents? Have we openly talked about this together, or have we avoided the questions?
- Have my spouse and I clearly defined our priorities for our time now that we're retired? What does it mean to grow closer in marriage as we age, yet have distinct identities and interests? What are the sources of conflict right now in our marriage, and what are the values underlying those conflicts?
- How much will I babysit for grandkids? And how much is too much? Do my kids know about these boundaries?

- In what way do I sense God calling me to make family a *vocation* in this season of life? Do I sense God's call to prioritize parents, children, or grandchildren in this season? Or do I sense God calling me to work, rest, volunteer, or serve other people's families?

Studies find that those who *write out* their plan for retirement are far more satisfied than those who don't.[11] Clearly written priorities and values can help to properly manage expectations and head off disappoint or frustration before it occurs.

Boundaries help to clearly define the things for which we are responsible, and the things for which other people are responsible. And boundaries that are clearly communicated set the stage for healthy family relationships.

Question our desire for independence

In one sense, independence is good and healthy. To be able to live, work, travel, and care for others until your dying day is the dream of many Americans.

Yet, on the other hand, most older adults say that being a "burden on family" is just as big a worry in retirement as money.[12] Tomes have been written about how deeply Americans prize their independence. Many of us shudder at the thought of *needing somebody else* as we age.

But this vision of unfettered independence is an illusion. From the time we're infants to the day we're on our death bed, we need others. We depend on others every day for food, water, and the very clothes on our back. Though properly launching adult kids on their own is good and healthy, we all must acknowledge that the day is coming when age means we will need others. Minimally, we need others well into old age because of our universal craving for human relationship.

On a chilly December day, Han Zicheng, an 85-year-old Chinese grandfather, gathered some scraps of paper and wrote, "Looking for somebody to adopt me."

Han taped his plea to a busy bus shelter in his neighborhood: "Lonely old man in his eighties. Strong-bodied. Can shop, cook and take care of himself. No chronic illness. I retired from a scientific research institute in Tianjin, with a monthly pension of 6,000 RMB [$950] a month," he wrote. "I won't go to a nursing home. My hope is that a kindhearted person or family will adopt me, nourish me through old age and bury my body when I'm dead."[13]

Han was desperate for company. His wife had died, his sons were out of touch, and his neighbors had kids and elderly parents of their own.

Han's story spread rapidly through social media. It highlighted a growing elderly population in China that is poor and lonely. China's one-child policy has caused a groundswell of adults over age 60—which is predicted to be nearly one in four by 2040—who don't have kids to care for them. Many saw the lonely Tianjin grandpa as part of a larger question that's spreading through the developed world: What is our responsibility toward those in old age? Is it the government's responsibility or the family's?

More specifically to those living in the US, what's our responsibility toward the 37 million Americans over age 50 living in economic uncertainty?[14] What if they happen to be our parents, aunts, uncles, or siblings?

What would it look like to quiet our desire for independence and move toward family and extended family in retirement who hunger for human connection and support? Might we start to take a more biblical view of family and embrace a sense of responsibility that extends from children and parents to the broader family of God (Matt. 12:50)?

COMMON:

Retirement is unfettered independence.

vs.

UNCOMMON:

In retirement, we can quiet our desire for independence and move toward family and extended family who hunger for human connection and support.

Our financial and time constraints are real, and God knows them well. Yet He also calls us to take up our cross and follow Him (Matt. 16:24). Sacrificial love, not personal independence, is our source of enduring joy. And it's the glue that holds together vibrant families.

Embrace the role of an elder

Elders are charged with becoming people filled with stories, wisdom, and blessing for their families and for generations to come.

When I was kid, I used to visit my Grandma Lonnie in Alexandria, Minnesota. She would make gingersnaps and banana bread. We would play the card game Spite and Malice, watch hummingbirds at her feeder, and snack on baked goods from her kitchen. Everything from shooting squirrels with a BB gun in her backyard to using her hand vacuum on the living room carpet was an adventure. As a child, my heart sang in her presence.

Now that Grandma Lonnie is gone, however, I long to know more of her stories. As an adult, I realized that many of them were too painful to tell to a child. My heart was wrenched the day I found out she was the victim of domestic abuse. As a child, my own father would go to local garage sales to buy her gifts with his allowance. Just to cheer her up.

Elders have a critical role to play in families. Kids and grandkids *need* their stories. They need to know where they came from and who they are. And it's only those who've been around long enough who can give that gift— the beautiful and the painful—to the next generation.

Christian faith is meant to be passed down. Those who possess it are "stewards of the mysteries of God" (1 Cor. 4:1 ESV) and called to "contend for the faith that was once for all entrusted to God's holy people" (Jude 3). Younger generations need baby boomers to share their stories, be caretakers of family memory, and humbly model what it means to be a Christ follower.

Caring for the spiritual nourishment of the next generation is a way to think about a deep vocation in retirement. If vocation means "one's entire life lived in response to God's call," vocation is big enough to encompass work, community service, and a long story on the front patio shared by Grandma, with milk, banana bread, and, of course, gingersnaps.

Legacy

Shannon Alder once wrote, "Carve your name on hearts, not tombstones. A legacy is etched into the minds of others and the stories they share about you."[15]

Retirement is the time to start being intentional about family legacy. What will weekends with Grandma look like? What do I want to share from my own life? What parts of Scripture have influenced my life—and what do my grandkids need to hear about my own faith journey? Practically, what does it mean for me to take my calendar and begin to plan out family dinners that will fulfill the psalmist's hope to "declare your [God's] power to the next generation, your mighty acts to all who are to come" (Ps. 71:18)?

One day, our family visited a cemetery near our house after church. We're so sheltered from death in our culture, I wanted our kids to simply take a walk and acknowledge their mortality, what most of history has considered a common fact of life. When we returned home for lunch, I asked my daughters what they wanted on their tombstone one day.

After a couple of the kids shared their ideas, Lily, my 7-year-old, gently said, "I want it to say, 'Lily was kind.'" The simplicity of this statement brought tears to my eyes. As I looked at her, I thought about Grandma Lonnie, who was exactly this: deeply, purely kind.

This was her legacy. Kindness.

Perhaps Lily will pass that legacy on to her kids and grandkids, and they too might pass on such peace and virtue even to "the children yet to be born" (Ps. 78:6).

Chapter 10

Hope

*"As the Father has sent me,
even so I am sending you."*

John 20:21 ESV

"What am I going to do with my retirement?"

With deep sincerity, Anne Bell's question is the same question that millions of baby boomers entering retirement are now asking. For many—including Christians—the question is often laced with fear, doubt, and uncertainty.

Fear. Americans approaching retirement often face fears about money, identity, and aging. Three in ten American adults don't have a penny saved for retirement.[1] Add in that many state-sponsored pension systems are nearing insolvency and healthcare costs are rising, the result is millions who wonder where their daily bread will come from as they age.

Others fear a loss of identity in retirement apart from professional accolades. While most 65-year-olds don't "feel" old, apprehension about irrelevance quietly clouds retirement parties with mugs that read "Good-bye tension, Hello pension."

Doubt. Those with sufficient savings tend to have deep questions about calling and purpose in retirement, fearing that a life of golf and Mai Tais won't lead to fulfillment. Deeper questions about calling, work, and rest are emerging from baby boomers who are uninterested in permanently "hanging up the cleats," yet are unclear about how to spend their time.

Uncertainty. The church has been nearly silent on the topic of retirement, except for a few voices who spurn retirement as not living for the glory of Christ. Yet after years of painful, unsatisfying labor, the mantra "Lord, spare me the curse of retirement!" rings hollow. Dream vacations, or just leaving work in the dust, sounds awfully good to many—even if it requires pushing back thoughts of a deeper purpose for one's golden years.

Yet not all face retirement with such apprehension. We've also seen that many embrace retirement, drawing from a deep well of life. Verona Mullison dives into learning about neuroplasticity as she considers the next steps in her life. Kent Johnson starts a consulting company to be an agent of reconciliation in corporate America. Barry Rowan takes a sabbatical rest and finds a renewed sense of inner peace. Susan Cole steps down from her role as a music teacher just in time to care for her family. Gene Veith retires but continues to write, teach, and travel to Scandinavia to share the gospel. Ellen Snyder volunteers at the St. Francis Center, a day shelter for the homeless. Rebecca Sahr writes down her plan for each week, knowing that each moment she's been given in retirement is a gift of grace.

None of these people have perfect circumstances. Health problems, money concerns, family problems, and vocational doubt often creep to the surface. But each person draws upon a deep reservoir of enduring hope for the next season of life.

HOPE FOR RETIREMENT

In everyday conversation, we often use the word *hope* to mean something like "wishful thinking" or "crossing your fingers for a long shot." For example, as a Minnesotan, I've often said, "I sure *hope* the University of Minnesota Gopher football team wins the national title." But inside I know I have a better chance of getting struck by lightning, bit by a shark, and winning the lottery on the same day. Hope is what's left over when plans have failed—and luck is needed.

But the biblical writers didn't use the word *hope* like this. Peter, for example, said God "has caused us to be born again to a living hope through the resurrection of Jesus Christ from the dead, to an inheritance that is imperishable, undefiled, and unfading" (1 Peter 1:3–4 ESV). Paul points to the "blessed hope"—the appearing of Jesus Christ at His second coming—as the foundation upon which believers stake their future (Titus 2:12–13). The biblical hope upon which the early church bet their very lives was that Christ would come again to judge and restore the world, and that the resurrection of Christ was the guarantee that we would one day be resurrected with Him as well. The biblical sense of hope is *complete trust* in God, for this life, for eternal life, and for the "life of the world to come."

For the Christian, retirement can be filled with a deep sense of purpose precisely because of this biblical hope.

The secular culture we live in struggles to find answers to "What's my purpose in retirement?" because it is based on a story that is itself emptied of hope. Our secular culture comes up with new "hopes" every day to satisfy our craving for meaning—whether those be new policies, products, or procedures—yet itself lives in a materialist story that sees humans as mere accidents of time and matter. We are just "dust in the wind," says Kansas in their famous 1977 song. "Nothing lasts forever but the earth and sky."[2] If we're just matter and molecules, then it's best to grab on to the fleeting pleasures of life or desperately try to make an impact before we're gone forever.

But the human longing for purpose suggests we *are* going somewhere. It's in the Christian story that the heart comes alive because it reveals that God Himself will return to the earth and restore all that has been broken. A joyful wedding feast with people from every tribe, tongue, and nation is the destiny of human history.

Retirement has hope only because the Christian story is true. "Behold, I am making all things new," Jesus says (Rev. 21:5 ESV). Hope is not a long shot. It's cluding your retirement.

> **COMMON:**
> **Fear, doubt, and uncertainty in retirement**
>
> **vs.**
>
> **UNCOMMON:**
> **Retirement has hope because the Christian story is true.**

Renewal

A TV commercial for Anacin, the pain reliever, says, "I like my job and am good at it, but it sure grinds me down sometimes, and the last thing I need to take home is a headache."

Many enter into retirement with great plans to pursue hobbies, visit family, or have a second career. But many also feel tired from a lifetime of work, like dust ground into fine powder. Many are searching for renewal in retirement, for God to breathe into their nostrils the breath of life once more (Gen. 2:7).

Yet how do we find such renewal for retirement?

We started to answer this by *questioning the contemporary culture of retirement.* We explored the history of the "Let's vacation" paradigm, from the Social Security Act of 1935 to Del Webb's Sun City. We also paused to

173

consider the economic challenges facing millions who will never be able to afford the never-ending retirement vacation. We saw the need for the church to find a deeper answer to retirement than "never stop working," and a way to find deep internal renewal before jumping into an encore career. The path to renewal begins with pausing to question the culture we're swimming in or to ask if there's another way.

Second, I argued that renewal for retirement needs not just a Sabbath day once a week, but a *true sabbatical*: an intentional three, six, or twelve months of worshipful rest, preparing the soul for a new season of creative service. Sabbath rest brings renewal by reorienting the heart to trust in God, find our identity in Him, and notice the vulnerable. A sabbatical is a way to structure time to heal the heart and listen for God's voice. Though the Bible suggests that one year off out of every seven is the best way to sustain a career over a lifetime, retirement is the first realistic time many have ever had to take any kind of extended period of rest and renewal.

Third, we said that a sabbatical is a perfect time to *reconsider your calling*. Many have the view that their calling will either be "my ideal job" or an inscrutable divine blueprint. Instead, we explored reengaging questions of calling in terms of the Great Commandment and how a sense of vocation changes over a lifetime. We asked some key questions to enable us to hear the voice of the Caller and make critical decisions about work, family, mentoring, and fruitful service.

Finally, we redefined *work not only as a means to compensation but an avenue for meaningful contribution.* Work is a way to love our neighbors. Though retirement is defined as "the action or fact of leaving one's job and ceasing to work," millions of baby boomers are rejecting the notion of a complete cessation of work for the final twenty to thirty years of life. Most are also ready to make a significant change in their working lives. Though work changes in retirement—and is not without its challenges—it is a means to serving others with the gifts God has entrusted to us (1 Peter 4:10).

According to John Stott, "work is the expenditure of energy . . . in the service of others, which brings fulfillment to the worker, benefit to the community and glory to God."[3] If this is true, work belongs in the life of every believer—even in retirement.

Wisdom

We also saw that core to a biblical view of aging is the concept of wisdom. Traditionally, the elders of a community were looked to for insight and wisdom to guide the community's decisions, spiritual life, and social integrity. Part II explored the idea of wise living from several angles:

- *Time*: using our newfound human longevity with intentionality;
- *Body*: honoring the "temple of the Holy Spirit" through healthy living, even while acknowledging the reality of the human condition;

- *Learning*: developing courage to explore new fields of human endeavor;
- *Mentoring*: raising a new generation of leaders through developing intergenerational friendships;
- *Family*: serving kids, grandkids, siblings, and aging parents as an expression of Christian vocation.

Rather than retreating into private life, biblical elders embrace their age as a season to influence their families, communities, and the broader society. To become an elder is to become a person of wisdom and blessing, adorned principally with the humility of Christ.

Dwight L. Moody has been credited with saying, "Preparation for old age should begin not later than one's teens. A life which is empty of purpose until 65 will not suddenly become filled on retirement." Though that's true, retirement is an opportunity to re-explore and then fulfill just such God given purposes for a new season of life.

Rested, Renewed, and Sent

Early on the first day of the week, Mary Magdalene went to the tomb of Jesus. She found the stone in front of the entrance had been rolled away. When she saw this, she frantically ran and told Peter and John that somebody had stolen Christ's body. In tears, Mary returned to the tomb with Peter and John. After they saw the empty tomb, the disciples left. But Mary stayed and wept outside the tomb just as the sun was rising on Sunday morning.

Suddenly, two angels appeared and asked her, "Woman, why are you crying?" "They have taken my Lord away, and I don't know where they have put him," she said, holding back sobs of grief. She then turned around and saw Jesus—but she didn't recognize Him. She thought He was the gardener since, after all, they were in a garden. And then Jesus called her by her name. He said simply, "Mary." Immediately, we she heard her name, she recognized Him and cried out "Rabboni!" Mary's new life began when the Savior called her by name.

One of my seminary professors once told me, "Jeff, the New Testament authors don't waste words. Pay attention to every one." In this passage, John the apostle carefully selects his words to draw parallels between the resurrection and the creation narrative in Genesis. Both the dawn of creation and the resurrection happen on the first day of the week. Both take place in a garden. And both culminate with an act of creation. Genesis tells the story of the first creation—the creation of humanity. John tells the story of *new creation*. In both stories, God breathes into His people the breath of life (Gen. 2:7; John 20:22). John is saying to his readers that the resurrection of Christ is the beginning of God's new world. Every believer now lives in the eternal dawn of the new heavens and earth.

Fear of impending aging, a failing body, social

isolation, and looming irrelevance haunts the minds of many entering retirement. In their minds at least, death is right around the corner, and this season of life seems to point toward that end. Yet Christianity gives us a very different story for retirement: one in which death and darkness have been conquered, and the resurrection of Jesus begins God's great plan to renew all things (Col. 1:15–20). Hope springs from the empty tomb and gives light to every corner of creation—including our families, work, neighborhoods, and cities.

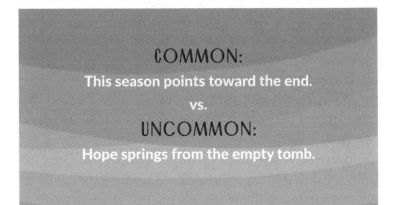

COMMON:

This season points toward the end.

vs.

UNCOMMON:

Hope springs from the empty tomb.

N.T. Wright writes about the resurrection, "Humans were made to reflect God's creative stewardship into the world. . . . [Jesus] laid the foundation, and we must build upon it. . . . Your task is to find the symbolic ways of doing things differently, planting flags in hostile soil, setting up signposts that say there is a different way to be human." To be "raised with Christ" is a creative calling to find ways our daily work and lives point beyond ourselves to Christ, the Light of the World.[4]

As you consider your calling for retirement, and recognize all the less-than-ideal circumstances that make up your life, take to heart Wright's advice, "Come to the Eucharist and see in the breaking of the bread the broken body of Christ given for the healing of the world. Learn new ways of praying with and from the pain, the brokenness, of that crucial part of the world where God has placed you."[5]

God calls all His people to live in union with Him, to bear witness to the gospel, and to serve the needs of the world with the work of their hands. The crucified Christ is risen. And He gently calls us to work alongside Him in the redemption of all things.

AND YOUR OLD MEN WILL DREAM DREAMS

A quote, often attributed to Antoine de Saint-Exupery, author of *The Little Prince,* goes like this: "If you want to build a ship, don't summon people to buy wood, prepare tools, distribute jobs, and organize the work. Instead, teach them to yearn for the vastness of the sea."[6]

What would it look like for the Christian church in America to transform our narrative about retirement? How might we move from leisure to love, from recreation to re-creation, from a life of self-focus to a love of service?

In light of the wisdom of the quote, the answer is not just to provide the proper financial tools for retirement but instead to cast a vision of a more beautiful life.

I'll return to the story of my friend Gary VanderArk.

Though Gary is approaching 80 years old and his body is slowing down, he is being ever renewed internally by God's spirit (2 Cor. 4:16). Gary is a man who teaches medical students, bicycles daily, sits on nonprofit boards, and advocates for the poor. And he is man who even came alongside me several years ago and encouraged me as I was launching Denver Institute for Faith & Work. It was Gary's gentle words spoken over my fragile plans that infused me with a deep, steady hope and confidence.

As I think of Gary's influence on my life, I'm reminded of the outpouring of the Spirit in Pentecost: "I will pour out my Spirit on all flesh, and your sons and your daughters shall prophesy, and your young men shall see visions, and your old men shall dream dreams" (Acts 2:17 ESV). It was Gary's renewed soul, his wisdom and blessing, and his embracing of the role of elder that gave me the confidence to accomplish the vision God gave to me. Like the prophets of long ago, Gary "dreamed dreams" and humbly passed to me the task of accomplishing my visions.

Retirement is a chance to pause and ask deeper questions about the next season of life. How will I spend my days? What is God calling me to? What will people say about me when I'm gone? What dreams will I dream over the next generation?

These questions may not have simple answers. But despite our limits and humanity, the resurrected Christ sees each of us and whispers, "As the Father has sent me, even so I am sending you" (John 20:21 ESV).

Afterword

"I never thought I would live to be this old," wrote Billy Graham at the ripe old age of 92. "All my life I was taught how to die as a Christian, but no one ever taught me how I ought to live in the years before I die."

When I read Dr. Graham's *Nearing Home—Life, Faith, and Finishing Well* upon its publication in 2011, I immediately had two reactions. First, I found that I had much greater empathy for my mom and dad who were in a similar season of life. Second, I felt a desire to help *all* people be prepared to experience more abundant lives before and during the final stages of their earthly race. *An Uncommon Guide to Retirement* has had a similar effect upon me.

This is a poignant topic for me because just this morning, I received a call notifying me that my beloved mother had entered through the gates of her heavenly home. Her life here came to an end as she peacefully breathed her final breath around 2:00 a.m. while in hospice care. She was eighty-four. Dr. Graham is gone. My mom is gone. I am entering the later third of my life as well.

This experience has only deepened my conviction that God is calling our generation to repurpose, not retire.

A CALL TO REPURPOSE NOW

The issues that Jeff has skillfully addressed are remarkably valuable. They bear significance to all audiences, whether young or old. He is challenging us to apply Psalm 90:12: "So teach us to number our days that we may get a heart of wisdom" (ESV). By becoming better stewards of the most precious and fleeting of all assets entrusted to us—our time on Earth—we can take hold of the life that is *truly* life and prepare for that day when we are absent from the body and present with the Lord (2 Cor. 5:8 KJV).

In response to Jeff's writings, to Scripture, and to the brevity of life, I urge all of us to move away from thinking of retirement and to reframe this season of life as a time to repurpose. Most of us will somehow pivot our career, and have available time to direct our energy, talents and experiences in a new direction.

BECOME AN ELDER, NOT ELDERLY

Our culture refers to older adults as "elderly or senior citizens"; the Bible refers to those godly examples with life experience as *elders*. Apart from a formal position in church governance, this title also denotes a position gained by wisdom that comes with a responsibility to serve as a model and mentor to those who are younger. It implies a purpose to pass along the life lessons that will aid those who desire to learn, grow, and become purposeful about their lives as well.

One of my friends repurposed his life at age 65. He and his wife were in great physical and spiritual shape. On his final day at work, during his farewell speech he said, "My wife and I have considered all of our options of how the Lord wants to use our remaining years. We have concluded that the highest and best use of our lives is to disciple our grandchildren and future great grandchildren. We want to invest our lives in them so they may grow in wisdom, stature, favor with God and man according to Luke 2:52."

And they were serious. They worked out a schedule with their three adult children to take the responsibility of spending time with their treasured grandchildren. They accomplished this by participating in their favorite activities, including them in their travels, and being deliberate about their Christian training at every age and stage of life. Can you imagine the dividends this will pay in this family both now and for eternity?

MAKE LIBERATING LIFESTYLE CHOICES

Well-meaning financial planners have told far too many older adults that they must have a very large nest egg to meet their retirement goals. Just plug in your numbers in those free, online calculators and find out how many millions your retirement account is probably lacking. What are omitted from the discussion are the lifestyle choices that can significantly alter your financial needs during your later years.

An Uncommon Guide to Retirement paints a picture

of living frugally, being generous, serving others, and trusting in God for our ultimate provision. Our freedom comes not from our finances, but from our riches in Christ.

WRITE YOUR NAMES ON THEIR HEARTS

Repurposing is becoming intentional about your legacy, as Jeff explains, "how you hope to be remembered." My favorite advice comes from Charles Spurgeon who advised, "Carve your name on hearts, not on marble."

God is love, and we are most like Him when we unconditionally love others. Regardless of your calling or vocation, all we do should be marked by sincere care and kindness toward everyone God has placed in our lives. The most touching funerals I have ever attended have been those where the audience is filled with people who have been touched by the deceased person's love.

My mother did not graduate from high school, she never had a career, and she was never in the public eye. But at her funeral, I have no doubt I will hear the stories of how she made others feel important and loved. She raised me with the saying, "Those who deserve your love the least need it the most." Her host of friends often included the outcast, the rejected, the wounded, those that were desperate for love. Because of her genuine love, her name is carved on their hearts, just as it is carved on mine.

As I enter the season of life I'm now seeing my parents finish, I want to repurpose my life for Christ and His kingdom, not retire.

I recognize this choice is "uncommon." But Christ's life was countercultural. And I pray my life in this next season of life too will point to the deep and lasting hope both my mother and I share.

I hope you'll join us.

CHUCK BENTLEY
CEO, Crown Financial Ministries

Acknowledgments

To be entrusted with someone else's story is to be given a precious gift. In the course of writing this book, I was entrusted with the hopes, fears, dreams, doubts, and desires of dozens of men and women looking to the future without clear answers. To each of you, named and unnamed, you have my deep gratitude.

I want to thank Amanda Cleary Eastep at Moody for her astute editorial eye and my friend Andrew Wolgemuth for believing in this project, my first trade book, to get it from concept to print.

I want to thank the board and staff of Denver Institute for Faith & Work for giving early feedback on this project, as well as committed friends in the faith and work movement such as Dave Strunk, Brad Hewitt, Matt Reynolds, Tim Macready, Amy Sherman, Chris Horst, Rob Moll, Luke Bobo, Greg Enas, Mark Roberts, and Joanna Meyer.

I want to thank my mom, Lynn Haanen, and my dad, Greg Haanen, for sharing their stories with me. This book is for you both. May you both experience in your retirement the life that is truly life.

I also want to thank my bride, Kelly Haanen, for giving me the space and time to think apart from (as much as I love them!) our four daughters. Kelly, as you know, my mind, spirit, and heart are revived by your daily graces. What would I be without you? (And next time, I won't steal the manuscript from you—I promise!)

Finally, I want to thank the ever-present God for gently carrying me each step of the way. Who can breathe new life into dry bones but You? You alone have the words of life. I look forward to seeing what You will do next.

**FOR MORE RESOURCES,
VISIT UNCOMMONRETIREMENT.COM.**

Notes

Part I: Renewal

Chapter 1—Culture

1. Marc Freedman, *Prime Time: How Baby Boomers Will Revolutionize Retirement and Transform America* (New York: Public Affairs, 1999), viii.
2. Glenn Kessler, "Do 10,000 baby boomers retire every day?" *Wall Street Journal,* July 24, 2014, https://www.washingtonpost.com/news/fact-checker/wp/2014/07/24/do-10000-baby-boomers-retire-every-day/?utm_term=.b8f3e33fe0b1.
3. "2010 Census Shows 65 and Older Population Growing Faster Than Total US Population," US Census Bureau, November 31, 2011, https://www.census.gov/newsroom/releases/archives/2010_census/cb11-cn192.html.
4. Wan He, Daniel Goodkind, and Paul Kowal, "An Aging World: 2015," United States Census Bureau, March 2016, https://www.census.gov/content/dam/Census/library/publications/2016/demo/p95-16-1.pdf.
5. "No Matter Your Age, Ignore It at Your Peril," *100 Year Life* website, http://www.100yearlife.com/the-challenge.
6. Elyssa Kirkham, "1 in 3 Americans Has Saved $0 for Retirement," *Time,* March 14, 2016, http://time.com/money/4258451/retirement-savings-survey.
7. Lee Barney, "People's Biggest Retirement Cost Concern Is Health Care," *Plan Advisor,* May 18, 2017, https://www.planadviser.com/peoples-biggest-retirement-cost-concern-is-health-care.
8. Nancy Cook, "Will Baby Boomers Change the Meaning of Retirement?" *The Atlantic,* June 28, 2015, https://www.theatlantic.com/business/archive/2015/06/baby-boomers-retirement/396950.
9. Caroline Parkinson, "Why Retirement Can Be Bad for Your Health," *BBC,* May 16, 2013, http://www.bbc.com/news/health-22553577.

10. "Baby Boomers: Religious composition of baby Boomers," Pew Research Center, http://www.pewforum.org/religious-landscape-study/generational-cohort/baby-boomer.
11. Freedman, *Prime Time*, 53–54.
12. Ibid., 37.
13. For a fascinating treatment of the history of retirement, see chapter 3, "A Year-Round Vacation," in Marc Freedman's *Prime Time* (New York: Public Affairs, 1999), 50.
14. Jenny Joseph, "Warning," *Jenny Joseph Selected Poems* (Hexham, UK: Bloodaxe Books Ltd., 1993), 42.
15. Chris Heath, "The Unbearable Bradness of Being," *Rolling Stone*, Issue 824, October 28, 1999, 72.
16. "Age may well wither them: Americans are not saving enough for retirement," *The Economist*, November 7, 2015, https://www.economist.com/news/finance-and-economics/21677661-americans-are-not-saving-enough-their-retirement-age-may-well-wither-them.
17. Cameron Huddleston, "What Social Security Will Look Like in 2035," July 20, 2018, https://www.gobankingrates.com/retirement/social-security/what-will-social-security-be-in-2035/#3.
18. Suzanne Woolley, "Most Americans Live in Fear of Retiring Poor," *Bloomberg*, February 28, 2017, https://www.bloomberg.com/news/articles/2017-02-28/retirement-anxiety-is-gripping-america.
19. John Mauldin, "Europe's Pension Funds Are Running Low as Boomers Retire," *Forbes*, July 2, 2018, https://www.forbes.com/sites/johnmauldin/2018/07/02/europes-pension-funds-are-running-low-as-boomers-retire/#329a34af63a0.
20. Mitch Anthony, *The New Retirementality*, Fourth Edition (New Jersey: Wiley, 2014), 16.
21. John Piper, *Rethinking Retirement* (Wheaton, IL: Crossway, 2009), 28.
22. Ibid., 6, 24.
23. Ralph D. Winter, "The Retirement Booby Trap," *Mission Frontiers*, July 1, 1985, http://www.missionfrontiers.org/issue/article/the-retirement-booby-trap.
24. Freedman, *Prime* Time, v.
25. "Retire? Seniors Want to Rejoin the Workforce," YouTube.com, DW English, published on February 18, 2015, https://www.youtube.com/watch?v=ZJJ8HT7_oLA.
26. Doug Groothuis, "Deposed Royalty: Pascal's Anthropological Argument," June 30, 2002, http://static1.1.sqspcdn.com/static/f/38692/206979/1262870209153/Deposed+Royalty+-+Pascals+A.

Chapter 2—Sabbath

1. Paula Span, "Many Americans Try Retirement, Then Change Their Minds," *New York Times,* March 30, 2018, https://www.nytimes.com/2018/03/30/health/unretirement-work-seniors.html.
2. *The Intern*, 2015, https://www.imdb.com/title/tt2361509.
3. Ibid.
4. Freedman, *Prime Time*, vi.
5. Craig J. Slane, "Sabbath," *Baker's Evangelical Dictionary of Biblical Theological*, Walter A. Elwell, ed. (Grand Rapids, MI: Baker Academic, 2001), https://www.biblestudytools.com/dictionaries/bakers-evangelical-dictionary/sabbath.html.
6. "State of American Vacation 2018," Project: Time Off, https://projecttimeoff.com/reports/state-of-american-vacation-2018.
7. "State of American Vacation 2018," Project: Time Off, https://projecttimeoff.com/wp-content/uploads/2018/05/StateofAmericanVacation2018.pdf, 5.
8. Gordon T. Smith, *Courage and Calling: Embracing Your God-Given Potential* (Downers Grove, IL: InterVarsity Press, 2011), 85.
9. Paul Johnson, *A History of the Jews* (New York: Harper & Row, 1987), 37.
10. Sabbatical is a term often used for extended time off for academics (and the occasional lucky pastor). But even in corporate America, the idea is gaining steam. In 2017, 17 percent of American companies had formal unpaid sabbatical programs, and 5 percent offered paid sabbaticals (Source: cnbc.com/2018/09/02/sabbaticals-for-skilled-employees). The idea of a full *year* of Sabbath rest is deeply biblical. One year out of every seven Israelites were instructed to let their crops lie fallow and not do any work. "For six years sow your fields, and for six years prune your vineyards and gather their crops. But in the seventh year the land is to have a year of sabbath rest" (Lev. 25:3–4). God promised to provide such a yield in the sixth year that they would have enough to eat until crops from the ninth year were harvested (25:22).

    In his book *Playing God: Redeeming the Gift of Power*, Andy Crouch asks a provocative question: What if our entire careers were marked by six years of work, and then one of rest—instead of putting all our years of rest on the back-end of our lives (retirement)? As it turns out, the math is pretty provocative. He writes, "If one were to start full-time work at twenty-one and retire at the age of sixty-nine, then hoped to enjoy an 'active retirement' until, say seventy-seven before being more constrained by the limitations of old age, the forty-eight years of work would be matched by eight years of retirement—exactly the 1-for-6 ratio of the sabbatical year." See Andy Crouch, *Playing God: Redeeming the Gift of Power* (Downers Grove, IL: InterVarsity Press, 2014).

11. Judith Shulevitz, *The Sabbath World: Glimpses of a Different Order of Time* (New York: Random House, 2011).

12. Lauren Winner, *Mudhouse Sabbath* (Brewster, MS: Paraclete Press, 2003), 11.

13. Adele Calhoun, *Spiritual Disciplines Handbook: Practices that Transform Us* (Downers Grove, IL: InterVarsity Press, 2005), 75.

14. One of the best treatments of simplicity is penned by Richard Foster. See: Richard Foster, *The Celebration of Discipline* (San Francisco: Harper & Row Publishers, 1978).

15. Jeff Haanen, "Michael Lindsay: Go Where Decisions are Made," *Christianity Today,* August 6, 2014, http://www.christianitytoday .com/ct/2014/august-web-only/michael-lindsay-you-have-to-be- in-room.html.

16. Norton Jester, *The Phantom Tollbooth* (New York: Random House, 1961), 124–25.

Chapter 3—Calling

1. Personal interview with Barry Rowan on September 13, 2016.

2. Kate Harris, "What We're Talking about When We Talk About 'Vocation,'" Q Ideas, http://qideas.org/articles/what-were- talking-about-when-we-talk-about-vocation.

3. Jeff Haanen, "What's wrong with 'do what you love?'", June 27, 2017, http://www.patheos.com/blogs/missionwork/2014/06/ whats-wrong-with-do-what-you-love/.

4. Gordin Marino, "A Life Beyond 'Do What You Love,'" *New York Times,* May 17, 2014, https://opinionator.blogs.nytimes .com/2014/05/17/a-life-beyond-do-what-you-love/?_php=true&_ type=blogs&_r=0.

5. Miya Tokumitsu, "In the Name of Love," *Jacobin,* January 12, 2014, https://www.jacobinmag.com/2014/01/in-the-name-of-love.

6. Os Guiness, *The Call: Finding and Fulfilling the Central Purpose of Your Life* (Downers Grove, IL: InterVarsity, 2003), 51.

7. Wendell Berry, *Jayber Crow* (Washington, DC: Counterpoint, 2001), 66. Emphasis mine.

8. Some, like Os Guinness, only make the distinction between primary calling and secondary calling. Here, primarily calling is focused on the love of God and neighbor, and a secondary calling is a specific task God gives to individuals.

9. Guinness, *The Call*, 19.

10. "Interview with Skye Jethani," Denver Institute for Faith & Work (video interview), Vimeo, https://vimeo.com/100166997.

11. Quoted in: William C. Placher, ed. *Callings: Twenty Centuries of Christian Wisdom on Vocation* (Grand Rapids, MI: Eerdmans, 2005), 283.

12. Albert Schweitzer, Charles Rhind Joy, *Albert Schweitzer: An Anthology* (Boston: Beacon Press, 1947), 157. eBook.

13. "George Washington Carver: God-glorifying Agricultural Innovator," League of Everyday Doxologists, http://www.doxologists .org/george-washington-carver-god-glorifying-agricultural-innovator. See also the wonderful, short biography of George Washington Carver: Glenn Clark, *The Man Who Talks to Flowers* (Austin, MN: Macalester Park Publishing Company, 2007).

14. Personal phone interview with Fred Smith on June 28, 2018.

15. Gordon Smith, *Courage and Calling* (Downers Grove, IL: InterVarsity Press, 2011), 98.

16. Ibid., 97.

17. These questions are adapted from Gordon Smith's wonderful little book: *Consider Your Calling* (Downers Grove, IL: InterVarsity Press, 2016).

18. Amy Sherman, *Kingdom Calling: Vocational Stewardship for the Common Good* (Downers Grove, IL: InterVarsity Press, 2011).

Chapter 4—Work

1. Robert Bellah, Richard Madsen, William M. Sullivan, Ann Swindler, and Steven M. Tipton, *Habits of the Heart: Individualism and Commitment in American Life* (Berkeley: University of California Press, 1985), 72.

2. Annamarie Mann and Jim Harter, "The Worldwide Employee Engagement Crisis," Gallup, January 7, 2016, http://news.gallup .com/businessjournal/188033/worldwide-employee-engagement-crisis.aspx.

3. Personal interview with Barry Rowan on September 15, 2017.

4. Drew Desilver, "More Older Americans Are Working, and Working More, than They Used To," Pew Research Center, June

20, 2016, http://www.pewresearch.org/fact-tank/2016/06/20/more-older-americans-are-working-and-working-more-than-they-used-to.

5. Glenn Ruffenach, "Want to work past retirement age? Here's the problem with that," Market Watch, September 19, 2017, https://www.marketwatch.com/story/want-to-work-past-retirement-age-heres-the-flaw-in-your-plan-2017-09-18.

6. Dorothy Sayers, *The Betrayal of Tradition: Essays on the Spiritual Crisis of Modernity*, Harry Oldmeadow, ed. (Bloomington, IN: World Wisdom, Inc., 2005), 221.

7. Timothy Keller, *Every Good Endeavor: Connecting Your Work to God's Work* (New York: Dutton, 2012), 63.

8. Elton Trueblood, *The Common Ventures of Life* (New York: Harper & Row, 1949), 87.

9. Gene Edward Veith, "Vocation in Retirement," *Tabletalk Magazine,* February 2018, https://tabletalkmagazine.com/article/2018/02/vocation-in-retirement.

10. "Ellen Snyder: Hope for Retirement (video)," *Denver Institute for Faith & Work,* April 2, 2015, https://denverinstitute.org/ellen-snyder-hope-for-retirement-video/.

11. Emily Brandon, "How Retirees Spend Their Time," *US News & World Report,* July 8, 2013, https://money.usnews.com/money/retirement/articles/2013/07/08/how-retirees-spend-their-time.

12. For more on the topic of "structural lag," see: Matilda White Riley, Robert L. Kahn, and Anne Foner, eds., *Age and Structural Lag: Society's Failure to Provide Meaningful Opportunities in Work, Family, and Leisure* (Hoboken, NJ: Wiley, 1994).

13. Richard Eisenberg, "Working In Retirement: Wishful Thinking?" *Forbes,* December 13, 2017, https://www.forbes.com/sites/nextavenue/2017/12/13/working-in-retirement-wishful-thinking.

14. Ben Steverman, "Working Past 70: Americans Can't Seem to Retire," *Bloomberg,* July 10, 2017, https://www.bloomberg.com/news/articles/2017-07-10/working-past-70-americans-can-t-seem-to-retire.

15. "I kept thinking: 'what is wrong with me?' — your experiences of ageism," *The Guardian,* April 28, 2017, https://www.theguardian.com/careers/2017/apr/28/i-kept-thinking-what-is-wrong-with-me-your-experiences-of-ageism.

16. For more on the growing class divide between those with a college education and those without, see: Jason Bellini, "Why

Deaths of Despair May Be a Warning Sign for America," *Wall Street Journal,* February 27, 2018, https://www.wsj.com/articles/why-deaths-of-despair-may-be-a-warning-sign-for-america-moving-upstream-1519743601.

17. Steverman, 1.

18. Doug Muder, "Not my father's religion," *UU World,* September 3, 2007, https://www.uuworld.org/articles/liberal-religion-the-working-class.

19. "Planning and Procrastination," *The Economist,* October 6, 2012, https://www.economist.com/schumpeter/2012/10/06/planning-and-procrastination.

20. *In Christ Alone* was written by Keith Getty and Stuart Townend, https://www.gettymusic.com/in-christ-alone.

21. Carole Fleck and David Wallis, "Next Career Act, Life Reimagined, for Boomers," *AARP magazine,* February/March 2015, https://www.aarp.org/work/working-after-retirement/info-2015/next-career-for-boomers.html.

22. Jeff Haanen, "How to Choose a Career: Advice from a Puritan Pastor," *Denver Institute for Faith & Work,* December 4, 2013, https://denverinstitute.org/how-to-choose-a-career-advice-from-a-puritan-pastor/.

23. Mother Teresa Quotes, Catholic Online, https://www.catholic.org/clife/teresa/quotes.php.

24. "Prophets of a Future Not Our Own," United States Conference of Catholic Bishops (website), http://www.usccb.org/prayer-and-worship/prayers-and-devotions/prayers/prophets-of-a-future-not-our-own.cfm.

25. Ibid.

26. As quoted in the *The British* Friend by Edward Grubb, Volumes 13–14, April, 1905, 93. According to sefaria.org, Pirkei Avot 2:16, the translation reads: "It is not your responsibility to finish the work, but neither are you free to desist from it."

Part II: Wisdom

Chapter 5 — Time

1. Dr. Seuss, *Oh, the Places You'll Go!* (New York: Random House, 1990), 24.

2. Lynda Gratton & Andrew Scott, *The 100 Year-Life: Living and Working in an Age of Longevity* (London: Bloomsbury, 2016), 1.

3. Dan Kadlec, "The Ages When Most People Retire (Hint: Probably Too Young)," *Time,* December 1, 2016, http://time.com/money/4584900/ages-people-retire-probably-too-young-early-retirement.

4. Gratton & Scott, *The 100 Year-Life: Living and Working in an Age of Longevity,* 4.

5. Ibid., 5.

6. Ibid., 9.

7. Ibid., 8.

8. Emily Brandon, "How Retirees Spend Their Time," *US News & World Report,* July 8, 2013, https://money.usnews.com/money/retirement/articles/2013/07/08/how-retirees-spend-their-time.

9. Steve Vernon, "How Watching Too Much TV Can Ruin Your Retirement," *CBS Moneywatch,* August 16, 2011, https://www.cbsnews.com/news/how-watching-too-much-tv-can-ruin-your-retirement.

10. Paul Graham, "Maker's Schedule, Manager's Schedule," http://www.paulgraham.com/makersschedule.html.

11. Charles Dickens, *A Christmas Carol and Other Stories* (New York: Modern Library, 2000).

Chapter 6—Health

1. "The Health and Retirement Study," National Institute on Aging, US Department for Health and Human Services, https://www.nia.nih.gov/sites/default/files/2017-06/health_and_retirement_study_0.pdf.

2. Personal interview with Hillary Lum, July 25, 2018.

3. "National Health Expenditures 2016 Highlights," Centers for Medicare and Medicaid Service, https://www.cms.gov/Research-Statistics-Data-and-Systems/Statistics-Trends-and-Reports/NationalHealthExpendData/downloads/highlights.pdf.

4. Niall Ferguson, *Civilization: The West and the Rest* (New York: Penguin, 2011), 191.

5. "National Health Expenditures 2016 Highlights,"PDF.

6. Abraham Nussbaum, *The Finest Traditions of My Callings: One Physician's Search for the Renewal of Medicine* (New Haven, CT: Yale University Press, 2016), 4–5.

7. St. Basil, "The Long Rules," questions 55, https://sites.google.com/site/stbasilasceticalworks/the-long-rules-1.

8. Ibid.

9. Bob Cutillo, *Pursuing Health in an Anxious Age* (Wheaton: Crossway, 2017), 154.

10. Ibid., 155.

11. Quoted in: Joel Schuman and Brian Volck, *Reclaiming the Body: Christians and the Faithful Use of Medicine* (Grand Rapids: Brazos Press, 2006), 46.

12. From early Gnosticism to some medieval monastic communities to some aspects of American fundamentalism, Greek dualism has been widely co-opted by the church through the ages.

13. Stephanie Cohen, "Romance and STDs: Inside Florida's wild retirees getaway," *New York Post,* January 25, 2009, https://nypost.com/2009/01/25/retire-to-the-bedroom.

14. George E. Vaillant, *Triumphs of Experience, The Men of the Harvard Grant Study* (Cambridge, MA: Harvard University Press, 2012), https://books.google.com/books?id=At8HS89GbPoC&printsec=frontcover&dq=Triumphs+of+Experience&hl=en&sa=X&ved=0ahUKEwjxnoCXss_eAhUByYMKHa2bAlYQ6AEIKjAA#v=onepage&q=Triumphs%20of%20Experience&f=false.

15. Ibid., chapter 9, 292.

16. Joan Chittister, *The Gift of Years* (New York: BlueBridge, 2008), 17–18.

17. Kerry Egan, *On Living* (New York: Riverhead Books, 2016), 7–8.

18. N.T. Wright, *Surprised by Hope* (San Francisco: HarperOne, 2008), 293.

19. Rodney Stark, *The Rise of Christianity: How the Obscure, Marginal Jesus Movement Became the Dominant Religious Force in the Western World in a Few Centuries* (HarperSanFrancisco, 1997), 73–94.

Chapter 7—Learning

1. Cicero, *On Old Age* (New York: P.F. Collier & Son Corporation, 1909), 58.

2. Ibid.

3. Norman Doidge, "Major Alzheimer's Breakthrough: 200 Patients Have Their Symptoms Reversed," September 4, 2017, http://www.normandoidge.com/?p=2140.

4. For more information, visit: https://www.roadscholar.org.

5. Jeff Haanen, "How Do We Change? Formation in the 5280 Fellowship," April 17, 2017, https://denverinstitute.org/how-do-we-change-formation-in-the-5280-fellowship.

6. For more information, visit: https://religiousdiversityatwork.com.

7. Cicero, 74.
8. Dietrich Bonhoeffer, *Letters and Papers from Prison* (Minneapolis: Fortress Press, 2010), 26.
9. Quoted in: Steven Garber, *Visions of Vocation* (Downers Grove, IL: InterVarsity Press, 2014), 13.
10. John Milton, *Of Education,* (New York: P.F. Collier & Son Corporation), 255. Also available online at: https://www.bartleby .com/3/4/1.html.

Chapter 8—Mentoring

1. C. S. Lewis, *The Four Loves* (San Francisco: HarperOne, 2017), Reissue edition, 78.
2. Steven Strott, "Intergenerational Friendship," Denver Institute for Faith & Work website, 9 November 2015, https://denverinstitute .org/intergenerational-friendship.
3. D. Michael Lindsay and James K. A. Smith, "The Hidden Curriculum of Leadership," *Comment Magazine,* May 8, 2014, https://www.cardus.ca/comment/article/the-hidden-curriculum-of-leadership/.
4. Friendship is also built upon supporting another's social identity. For more on this topic, see: Karen Karbo, "Friendship: The Laws of Attraction," *Psychology Today,* November 1, 2006, https://www.psychologytoday.com/us/articles/200611/ friendship-the-laws-attraction.
5. For an excellent treatment on vulnerability, authority, and leadership, see: Andy Crouch, *Strong and Weak* (Downers Grove, IL: InterVarsity Press, 2016).
6. D. Michael Lindsay and James K. A. Smith, "The Hidden Curriculum of Leadership."
7. Robert Putnam, *Our Kids* (New York: Simon & Schuster, 2015), 190.
8. Ibid., 259.
9. Linda Gorman, "Is Religion Good for You?" The National Bureau of Economic Research, http://www.nber.org/digest/oct05/ w11377.html.

Chapter 9—Family

1. "Growing Old in America: Expectations vs. Reality" Pew Research Center, June 9, 2009, http://www.pewsocialtrends .org/2009/06/29/growing-old-in-america-expectations-vs-reality.

2. "Americans Re-Set Retirement Expectations," The Retirement Re-Set Study: AIG, https://www-1000.aig.com/TridionData .do?Page_ID=355474.

3. "Family Support in Graying Societies," Pew Research Center, May 21, 2015, http://www.pewsocialtrends.org/2015/05/21/ family-support-in-graying-societies.

4. "Led by Baby Boomers, divorce rates climb for America's 50+ Population," Pew Research Center, March 9, 2017, http://www .pewresearch.org/fact-tank/2017/03/09/led-by-baby-boomers- divorce-rates-climb-for-americas-50-population.

5. Anthonia Akitunde, "How Retirement Can Hurt Your Marriage (And What You Can Do About It)," *Huffington Post,* August 9, 2013, https://www.huffingtonpost.com/2013/08/09/divorce-after- 50-retirement_n_3286342.html.

6. Patrick Sisson, "How intergenerational living benefits the 'book-end' generations," *Curbed,* June 8, 2018, https://www .curbed.com/2018/6/8/17442710/senior-living-multigenerational- intergenerational.

7. "All In Together: Creation Places Where Young and Old Thrive," Generations United, https://www.gu.org/resources/all- in-together-creating-places-where-young-and-old-thrive.

8. Patrick Sisson, "How a return to multigenerational living is shifting the housing market," *Curbed,* November 2, 2017, https:// www.curbed.com/2017/11/21/16682850/multigenerational- homes-millennials-immigration-family.

9. "Family Support in Graying Societies," Pew Research Center.

10. "Family & Retirement: The Elephant in the Room," Age Wave, http://agewave.com/what-we-do/landmark-research-and- consulting/research-studies/family-retirement-the-elephant-in- the-room.

11. Akitunde, "How Retirement Can Hurt Your Marriage (And What You Can Do About It)."

12. "Family & Retirement: The Elephant in the Room," Age Wave.

13. Emily Rauhala, "He was one of millions of Chinese seniors growing old alone. So he put himself up for adoption," *The Washington Post,* May 2, 2018, https://www.washingtonpost .com/world/asia_pacific/he-was-one-of-millions-of-chinese- seniors-growing-old-alone-so-he-put-himself-up-for- adoption/2018/05/01/53749264-3d6a-11e8-912d-16c9e9b37800_ story.html?utm_term=.6fef756106eb.

14. "The Unexpected Face of Poverty," *The Atlantic*, AARP, https://www.theatlantic.com/sponsored/aarp-2018/the-unexpected-face-of-poverty/1913.
15. Quoted in: David Cassidy, "Is Your Legacy Etched in the Minds of Others?", March 8, 2015, http://pastordavidcassidy.com/is-your-legacy-etched-in-the-minds-of-others.

Chapter 10—Hope
1. Elyssa Kirkham, "1 in 3 Americans Have \$0 Saved for Retirement," https://www.gobankingrates.com/retirement/planning/1-3-americans-0-saved-retirement.
2. Kansas, "Dust in the Wind," *Point of Know Return* (album), Kirshner, 1977, www.kansasband.com/discography.php.
3. John R. W. Stott, Roy McCloughry, and John Wyatt, *Issues Facing Christians Today* (Grand Rapids, MI: Zondervan, 2006), 225.
4. N.T. Wright, *The Challenge of Jesus: Rediscovering Who Jesus Was and Is* (Downers Grove, IL: InterVarsity Press, 2015), 184, 186.
5. Ibid., 191.
6. "Teach Them to Yearn for the Vast and Endless Sea," Quote Investigator, https://quoteinvestigator.com/2015/08/25/sea.

IT'S NOT JUST ABOUT THE MONEY...

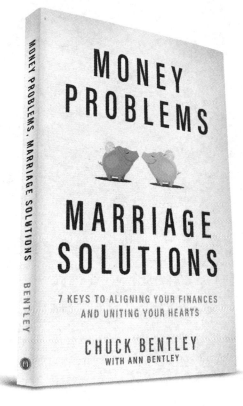

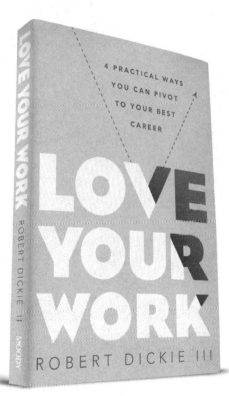

HOW TO MAKE EVERY DOLLAR COUNT IN ANY FINANCIAL CLIMATE

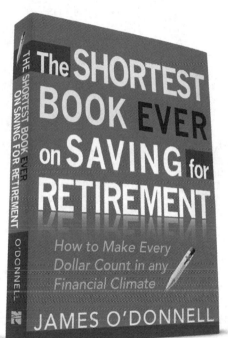

978-0-8024-4653-4 | also available as an eBook